The Source Book of Hindu Mythology, (2nd Edition)

By Dr. Krishna R. Sarma

ISBN-10:0-9882687-5-2

ISBN-13:978-0-9882687-5-3

Cover design by

JC Polk, II, Richmond, VA

Illustrations by

Osumz, a full service design firm

www.osumz.com

Edited by

Bettie Duke Sarma

Published June 2017

The author's comments are italicized.

Publisher
Ebookmarketingplus.com LLC
Richmond, Virginia

Table of Contents

3

4

9

11

13

Dedication

This book is dedicated to my late wives;

Inge who suggested first writing this book and

Meena who supported with a great deal of enthusiasm.

May their memories last much longer than their lives.

Foreword

"Hindu Mythology" is usually understood as the story of the two great epics, the Rāmāyana and Mahābhārata. This is only partly correct as the mythology itself is comprised of many events, actions, and effects of those actions by the gods and demons (Devas and Dānavas). How did it all happen? It started as the origin of the universe created by Brahma at the urging of Vishnu. It is connected intricately with time, specifically four different periods called Yugas. A Yuga is a measure of mythological time in Hinduism according to which Vishnu will appear from time to time to establish Dharma or world order. There are four Yugas in which Dharma is established on a firm foundation or principles. Dharma itself has the conceptual form of a four-legged animal very similar to a buffalo. The lord of the netherworld Yama, who also enforces Dharma, rides on a buffalo. The first of the Yugas is the Krutha Yuga, which lasts, according to human years for 1,728,000 years and in which Dharma is strong and actually stands on four feet (or four legs). Next comes Trētha Yuga which lasts for 1,296,000 years in which Dharma is only three footed, so injustice (Adharma) takes hold and even grows. Then comes Dwāpara Yuga that lasts for 864,000 years and during which Dharma stands only on two feet. Dwāpara Yuga is followed by Kali Yuga which lasts for 432,000 years and Dharma stands on only one foot.

A Mahāyuga is the sum of all the four Yugas, which means it will last for a period of 4,320,000 years. A Kalpa, on the other hand, is comprised of 1,000 Mahāyugas, which is the cycle for Brahma (or the creator) to recreate the Earth. The age of the Earth if we consider it approximately as a Kalpa would be 4.32 billion years. If we compare this with the age of the Earth as calculated from thermodynamics and heat conduction, it is 4.23 billion years. Does this mean we have only about 900,000,000 years left? Maybe after all the recent astronomical data and its predictions tell us the Sun would begin to cool off in about 900 million years.   A sheer coincidence or is there something to it?

At the end of each Kalpa, the universe dissolves in a deluge out of which the creator recreates the whole universe either according to the old model or a new one.   There is no form to distinguish between the old and the new, because the memory of the old one is not preserved.   One such occasion was when Vishnu asked Brahma to create the universe; he himself was floating on a mysterious liquid substance.   Brahma did not know what should be done, so he entered the womb of Vishnu to find out what it was the universe should consist of.   As it happened when Brahma was inside Vishnu, he closed all the orifices and a trapped Brahma had to come out of the navel of Vishnu. When he came out, Brahma had the full knowledge of what to create and how. He is considered to be the son of Vishnu because of this and soon after emerging from Vishnu, he was telling Vishnu that there was no one greater than them at which instant Shiva appeared and Vishnu paid respects to Shiva. A surprised Brahma listened carefully to Vishnu's narration of Shiva. At the first attempt, Brahma created the Sanatkumāras and asked them to expand the creation. They refused which angered Brahma and out of this were born the eleven Rudras. This was the first protest and exhibition of anger at the highest echelons! He then created the Prajāpatis who extended the creation as ordered. The word Prajāpati means literally lord of the people. Out of the moods of Brahma came a variety of beings such as the Devas, the Dānavas (demons), the Yakshas, and the Gandharvas. As these entities all needed space to live, Brahma created Viswakarman who built the physical world and universe.

Hindu Mythology is built around a concept of conservation; be it conservation of soul, time, or position. If for any reason one is lost, he is revived again in a different form. This is essentially reincarnation. One can lose a position as in the case of Jaya and Vijaya, the gatekeepers of Vishnu. Jaya and Vijaya were granted the option of either three lives as enemies of Vishnu or seven lives as friends. They chose three lives as enemies as this would allow them to return as soon as possible to their position. Choices were thus given even in punishment. The gods and the demons, they all had feelings similar to some of our own such as anger, love, greed, jealousy, and pity. They fall in love at first sight. They go through plotting, conniving, and many such intrigues to achieve their goals. In all of these, it is the Dharma that controls how justice is done with the perpetrator punished. Indra is a good example of this; he fell in love with Ahalya and schemed to seduce her. When he was caught, he was cursed by Ahalya's husband Gautama. Even the curse shows a certain sarcasm and compassion; Indra's body is covered with what he came for, namely vaginas, but they appear to others as eyes.

The powers of Gods are not limited only to them;

they can be acquired by others, even demons and the Asuras. The only way to acquire these powers is to pray and please the highest of the Gods, either Vishnu or Shiva or Brahma. The process by which this can be achieved is performing tapas, a combination of meditation, discipline, and self-sacrifice. This is a grueling procedure, but those who have accomplished it can ask the Gods for anything they wanted except immortality. The first impression is to use these powers to gain control of the worlds and torture the former enemies. But that is not always true. Some use these powers to accomplish good things, for example Bhagiratha performed tapas to restore his ancestors to the heavens; and Viswāmitra used them to achieve the status of a Brahmarshi.

Intensity of performing tapas, is in itself awesome. When someone is torturing one's self and dedicates his thoughts with utter concentration about the gods, the so called "heat" is felt by the Devas. This can be described in a way as the recent example of our times when Gandhi went starving or Satyagraha (meaning true anger at the injustice perpetrated), the world felt a kind of heat and began to react to nullify it. In such a case by granting the wish of the person performing the tapas. The question arises, who has such powers to grant those wishes? Obvious answer is not every one, only the three highest Gods and creators of the universe Brahma, Vishnu or Shiva.

Dedication to duty is regarded very highly. The great Pativratas acquire such eminence because of their dedication to their husbands. Their powers were such that they could even control the highest gods. Anasūya possessed the power to convert Brahma, Vishnu and Shiva into little children. Many such instances are told; then how could these Pativratas acquire those powers? The explanation may lie in the acceptance of the fact that discharging one's duties with dedication is the highest form of performance. This is also the essence of Bhagavadgīta when Krishna tells

Arjuna to do just his duty. Thus Pativratas can even order the Sun not to rise in order to protect their husbands, and the Sun has no choice but to oblige because of respect to a higher moral authority. Such an authority comes from dedication to duty with unwavering conviction.

In Hindu Mythology, one may encounter sudden love feelings and even instant births. These clearly cannot be explained in the modern sense, but an equivalent can be found in the mythology of the Greeks. A child grows immediately to manhood as Vyāsa did, and the virginity of the mother remains in tact. This is difficult to explain but its acceptance can be facilitated by recognizing powers beyond our laws of physics and biology. The speed of an object is expressed in terms of speed of wind (Vāyu Vega) or speed of thought (Mano Vega). Although scientifically the maximum speed an object can acquire is that of light, the fact we can imagine and conceive activity on distant planets and the Universe, is an indirect proof of Mano Vega. In such cases as the planets that are light years away, can be imagined of their activity, in a split second, makes Mano Vega infinite or extremely high. This was the case with Einstein, Sagan, Chandrasekhar, and such. Not every one could have such a talent; only a few gifted ones and that perhaps could be the case with such rishis as Vyāsa and Vālmiki. Even the great poet Kālidāsa was illiterate well into his manhood and a sudden miracle by Kāli gave him his talent, so also was Vālmiki who was an illiterate hunter before he became a Mahārishi.

In Hindu Mythology we encounter many peculiar beings such as Hanumān, who was a monkey but a wise and strong one with unparalleled strength. There were also some in the form of birds such as the great Jatāyu who fought Rāvana. These beings were also able to converse with humans and communicate with the Devas. Perhaps there is something profound in all this, the universe and its ecosystem as created has a built in equality and a predestined end. The end too is not a real end, because the system is conservation bound. Thus only the form and shape may change but not the intrinsic force. Simple is better than complex, asceticism is better than luxury and comfort, as in the case of Shiva who is the ultimate ascetic and whose abode Kailas, is high up in the cold Himalayan mountains, compared to Vishnu who is surrounded by luxury and comfort and whose abode Vaikunth is somewhere lower than Kailas but is comprised of cool lakes, massive gates, and luxurious gardens, etc. Also many Devas are surrounded by comfort and luxuries along with their spouses, whereas many rishis live in modest ashrams seeking and espousing knowledge, training pupils in finding the truth and the secrets of the universe. Knowledge and wisdom are always placed higher than brut strength and power. Viswāmitra was a powerful king but he wanted to become a Brahmarshi, so he renounced his kingdom and all comforts and began tapas to acquire the status of a Brahmarshi. He wanted recognition from none other than Vasishta who was his model as well as his rival.

All of the Devas ride animals called Vāhanas for their mobility. Vishnu rides an eagle called Garuda or Garudavāhana. Shiva's Vāhana is a bull called Nandi. Indra rides on a either a white elephant called Airāvata or on a white horse named Uchhaiswara. The great Ganesha sits on a mouse, his brother Kumāraswamy rides a peacock. Brahma rides on a swan and Agni on a goat. There is a common connection in all of these rides; the shape of a Deva or a God is mystical and varied but all their Vāhanas are earthly identifiable animals and most of them are also gentle. The powerful should not trod on the less powerful, but show a sense of togetherness albeit that of a master and servant. The servant is always dedicated to the master and thus regarded also as a deity. There are many Devas and Dānavas, but only the important ones enter the mythology; they come several times in various forms and stages. For example both

Indra and Surya (Sun) were the fathers of Sugrīva and Vāli in Rāmayana, and of Arjuna and Karna in Mahābhārata; and in both times it was Indra's son who killed Surya's son and also in both cases in a deceitful way. Thus a kind of predestination controls the end of a stage or an era. That is the essence of Hindu Mythology.

This book actually describes the figures of the Hindu Mythology, why they came and what they have done. It is not the author's intention to offer any commentary or explanation. That is the philosophical part and it is not attempted here. This work is primarily intended for the second generation of Indian-Americans who may not have the ready accessibility of Indian mythology as their parents had, through stories, narratives and even actual reading of the Purānas in their youth in the home country. The second generation has definitely heard many of the names and even able to correlate a few figures. However, a compendium such this is not available for a quick reference, and that need is considered satisfied in this book. Some names and even narratives may have a different slant other than that was expressed in this book, and that is because India is a very large country with some sixteen different variations of the main culture, each describing some events and figures in slightly a different form. This is also due to the fact that when translated from Sanskrit, some of the flowery expressions and their rhythmical character were interpreted as permitted by the capability of the language into which it was translated. It may even be the case in this book, because it too has restrictions of language, pronunciation, and form of expression. If there are any inaccuracies, it will be greatly appreciated if they were brought to the author's attention. I hope the readers would find this work satisfying their curiosity of Hindu Mythology and its figures and tales. May it serve in microcosm similar purpose as the great rishis Mārkandeya, Vālmiki, and Vyāsa intended.

The primary source of information for this book

comes from Mahabhrata, Ramayana, and Bhagavatam. Other Puranas consulted were Markandeya, Shiva, Vishnu and Brahma. Most of these were consulted for cross-reference purposes. Except for some parts of Ramayana and Mahabharata, which were referenced in the Sanskrit language, a large amount of information came from translations of the originals and also from a compendium authored by V. Srinivasa Rao under the Title "Purvagadha Lahari" (Stories of Old History), published in Telugu in 1992.

~K.R. Sarma

Pronunciation Of Proper Names

It is very difficult to pronounce the proper names of Indian Mythology as correctly. This is because some sounds, especially elongated sounds, are synthesized by spelling them differently. Such a synthesis can be achieved either by repeating the same vowel or using a symbol on the vowel to distinguish it from the ordinary or short form. The later is chosen to affect the correct pronunciation and it is expanded below with examples.

Vowels

a pronounced as the "u" in cut or but

ā pronounced as elongated "a" as in father

I pronounced as "I" in sit or bit

ī pronounced as elongated "I'" as the "ee" in seen, been, etc.

u pronounced as "u" in put

ū pronounced as elongated "u" as in crude or prudent

e pronounced as "e" in bet or set

ē pronounced as elongated "e" as in gate or mate

i pronounced as the "I" in site or bite

o pronounced as "o" in so or go

ō pronounced as elongated "o" as in stone or

whole

au pronounced as "ou" in shout or bout

Consonants

Sanskrit is a language whose sounds use the mouth muscles systematically and uniformly. <u>The consonants start with gutturals, sounds from the throat and the tongue:</u>

'k' as in kill, kim, etc.

'kh' as in inkhorn, bunkhouse

'g' as in god, give

'gh' as in baghot, loghouse

'gn' does not exist in English. The closest is that as in signature

<u>Then sounds from the tongue touching the back of the roof of the mouth:</u>

'c' as in church

'ch' as the combined sound of church hall

'j' as in jug, judge

'jh' as in the combined sound of hedge hopper

'jn' again this does not exist in English, nor can be synthesized. Closest is jha

<u>Sounds from tongue touching the front roof of the mouth:</u>

't' as in tea, touch

'th' as in anthill

'd' as in dog

'dh' as in redhead

'n' does not exist in English. Closest is nna

<u>Sounds from tongue touching the upper teeth:</u>

't' as the 'th' sound in pith

'th' as the 'th' in think

'd' as in the russian word da meaning yes

'dh' as the harsh sound of 'd'

'n' as in nun

Sounds from the lips:

'p' as in put, pot

'ph' as the 'ph' in shepherd

'b' as in bag, big

'bh' as in abhor

'm' as in mom

Then sounds that have no hard sound:

'y' as in young

'r' as in rod

'l' as in love

'v' as the 'w' in way

's' has no equivalent. Closest is 'sh' with light 'h' as in German Grashof.

'sh' as in shut

'sa' as in some

'h' as hut, hum

'la' as the 'l' sound in south Texas

'ksh' as spelled

Glossary

Many Sanskrit words have a distinct meaning that is sometimes difficult to explain, but is accepted in the English usage because of conceptual inference. For example, the word "Ashram" is now accepted as a place of serenity and meditation. Similarly, "Mantra" is something to chant and practice to achieve a certain goal. Although it is difficult to describe the full meaning, an explanation of frequently used words is presented in this glossary.

Akasa: Sky. Also implies space from which lights, sounds, and even some Devas appear suddenly to rescue a disciple or a victim.

Apsara: Heavenly maiden born from churning the oceans by Devas and Asuras. Important ones include Rambha, Urvasi, Tilottama, Menaka, and Ghrutachi. They are unmarried and perform dances, music, etc. to please the Devas. They are controlled by Indra, who deploys them to distract rishis from performing their rituals.

Ashram: A serene place where people go to seek knowledge, learning, meditation, and rituals under the guidance of a rishi or maharishi.

Astra: Weapon. Brahmastra – a weapon influenced by Brahma; Nagastra – a weapon influenced by Nagas (snakes), and such.

Asuras: Children of Kasyapa and Diti. They are constantly in rivalry with their cousins the Devas.

Āyudha: Weapon delivery system such as bow and arrow, sword, gada, etc. Astra can only be delivered by means of an Ayudha. Indra's āyudha was Vajra, Krishna's was Chakra, Arjuna's was Gandiva, Bhima's was Gada, and so on.

Brahma: One of the three principal deities Brahma, Vishnu, and Shiva. There are also four Brahmas born from different parts of Brahma.

These are Pulastya from his ear, Pulaha from his navel, Daksha from his thumb, and Narada from his thigh.

Brahmin: Caste of priests, scholars, and learned men. There were four castes: Brahmin, Kshatriya, Vaisya, and Sudra. Kshatriyas were kings, rulers, and generals. Vaisyas were mercantile class, and Sudras were all others such as farmers, builders, blacksmiths, and stonemasons.

Devas: Children of Kasyapa and Aditi. They ruled the heavens but were often defeated and conquered by Asuras.

Dik: Directions such as East, West, North, and South.

Dikpalaka: Ruler of a Dik. There are eight such rulers: Indra for East, Varuna for West, Kubera for North, and Yama for South. Agni (Fire) for Southeast, Chandra (Moon) for Northeast, Vayu

(Air) for Northwest, and Surya (Sun) for Southwest.

Diksha: Disciplined self-denial of comforts.

Gana: Followers or attendants as an entourage of Gods.

Graha: Planetary body. There are nine Grahas; seven after whom each day of the week is named, plus two additional Rāhu and Ketu.

Graha(2): Planet and also a demon. For example Rāhu and Ketu are demonic grahas, whereas Sun, Moon, Mars, Jupiter, Venus, etc are planets after which days of the week are named. There are nine Grahas.

Grahana: Eclipse; Chandra Grahana (Lunar) and Surya Grahana (Solar).

Guna: Attribute, characteristic.

41

Guru: Teacher, learned person, and an authority in his field. Guru is also a title that is given only after producing a pupil. Pupil is called "Sishya", a learned person who imparts knowledge and wisdom.

Himsa: Harmful, harming someone.

Janma: Birth, life. Purva Janma means previous life.

Karma: Fate. Religious ritual duty such as cremation.

Pativrata: A woman who devotes all of her time, work, and actions to please her husband. These women have miraculous powers obtained through devotion to their husbands.

Rishi: A wise man who received extraordinary powers through meditation, self-discipline, and prayer. Maharshi - a great rishi. Brahmarshi - Brahmin rishi. Rajarshi - Kshatriya rishi.

Tapas: Concentrated meditation with prayer and detachment of all comforts and needs to please the Gods. When the God is pleased, he will appear and grant the wishes of the person performing tapas.

Abhimanya

Abhimanya was the son of Arjuna and Subhadra. He was a great warrior especially with a bow and arrow on a chariot.

When Arjuna was spending a year in anonymity and unrecognized at the palace of Virāta, Abhimanya was also there. On the occasion when Arjuna helped defeat the enemies of Virāta, Virāta was so pleased that he asked Arjuna to marry his daughter Uttara. Arjuna said he could not marry her because he was already married, but offered Abhimanya to marry Uttara. Soon after their marriage, the Great War broke out between the Kauravas and the Pāndavas. Abhimanya displayed enormous talent as a warrior and defeated several older established warriors of the enemy ranks. One day when Drōna was commander of the Kauravas, he organized his armies in a Lotus Formation Padma Vyūha, which is very difficult to penetrate. Abhimanya knew how to penetrate it, but did not know how to escape from it. His uncles and other Pāndavas encouraged him to go in and they would come to his aid at the appropriate time. Abhimanya went in and was ferociously fighting the enemies. The enemy ranks consisted of such greats as Karna, Drōna, and Krupa. The boy was fighting bravely and tenaciously, but also getting tired and the promised help did not come. It was soon over when Karna crippled his chariot, Krupa destroyed his horses, and Abhimanya was forced to fight on foot. In hand-to-hand combat, he was alone and no match for the more established and experienced warriors. Within minutes the enemy force had defeated him.

Abhimanya had a son named Parīkshit who later became king.

Aditi

Aditi was the daughter of Daksha and Dharani (Earth) and the wife of Kasyapa. She had rivals such as Diti, Kadru, and Vinata who were also wives of Kasyapa. All of the devas were the children of Aditi just as all of the children of Diti were demons. One day when Kasyapa was visiting her, she told him how the children of Diti were constantly harassing her children. He gave Aditi a mantra and asked her to worship Vishnu. When she did, Vishnu appeared before her and told her he would become her son. That son was Vāmana (incarnation as a dwarf) who crushed Bali and restored the heavenly kingdom to Indra. When Diti was expecting a powerful son, Aditi was afraid and begged her son Indra to destroy Diti's child. Indra went into Diti's womb and tried to destroy the fetus but could not. (see Indra)

The children of Diti were called Daityas and they were always quarreling with the children of Aditi. Aditi was unhappy with this situation, so she prayed to the Sun and asked for a son to defeat the Daityas. The Sun granted her wish and she became pregnant, but was still fasting and performing all the rituals. When asked by Diti why she was starving the child inside her, Aditi became angry and pushed the child out of her womb. The child did not die and instead became a Sun called Martānda. Aditi also gave birth to

45

twelve Suns, the Adityas.

Agastya

Agastya was one of the great and prominent rishis and a long time bachelor. On one of his trips he found three bodies hanging upside down. When Agastya asked why the bodies were hanging, the bystanders replied that one of their descendants was unmarried and so had no children, thus preventing them from their future lives. Agastya realized that they were his ancestors and so he decided he must marry. He approached the king of Vidarbha and asked for the hand of his daughter Lopāmudra. When the king hesitated, his daughter came forward and agreed to marry Agastya. They were married and Lopāmudra bore him a son Druddhāsya, thus allowing Agastya's ancestors their future lives.

When Lopāmudra asked for some nice clothes and jewelry, Agastya went to several kings and asked for any money that was unused. One after another said they didn't have excess monies. They advised him to go to Ilvala who was very rich. When Agastya approached him, Ilvala respectfully offered him hospitality and served him goat meat. This was no ordinary goat, it was his brother Vātapi. When called out by name, Vātapi came out of the stomachs of people who had eaten him, thus killing the guests. Agastya knew this trick, so soon after the meal he rubbed his belly and uttered "digest Vātapi digest". Ilvala pretended he didn't know anything of this trick and gave Agastya lots of spare money.

46

Brahma came to Agastya and asked him to marry the daughter of Kavera who was furiously praying and carrying out tapas. When Agastya agreed to marry her, she said she was going to become a river. Agastya married her anyway and put her in his kamandala (a special copper pot) and gave it to his disciples for safekeeping until his return from the south. One drop from this kamandala became Lopāmudra and after Agastya married Lopāmudra, Kavera's daughter became a river. This river is called Kāveri.

Vindhya Mountain was competing with Himālaya and grew continuously, finally obstructing the movements of the Sun and the Moon. When other rishis asked Agastya to handle the problem, he came to Vindhya and said "I have to go south and I am too old to climb your magnificent height". Vindhya replied "I will bend and shrink so you can walk over me and I shall stay like that until you return". Agastya never returned, so the Vindhya is still bent and shorter than Himālaya.

The demons of the seas were terrorizing the earth and hiding in the sea after their terrorist acts. When requested by the rishis and the Devas, Agastya drank the seas dry and exposed the demons who were then slain. He was unable to refill the seas, which were filled later by Ganga through the efforts of Bhagīratha.

In the great fight between Rāma and Rāvana, Rāma lacked a chariot and arrows and was distressed at Rāvana's pounding. Agastya then taught Rāma the mantra of Adityahrudayam (Sun's Blessing). With that Rāma gained a chariot with astras (weapons) and conquered Rāvana.

Agni

A great brahmin called Viswānara prayed to Shiva for a son. His wife Suchi bore him a son called Vaiswānara. Astrologers said the boy's life would be at risk when he turned twelve years old. Viswānara went out and prayed to Shiva continuously. When Indra appeared and asked him about his wish, he refused saying "I am praying to Shiva, not you". This answer angered Indra and he struck Vaiswānara with his weapon Vajra. Shiva appeared immediately and blessed Vaiswānara with a long life. Vaiswānara became lord of the Southeast (Agneya). Agni is also the bearer of offerings to Gods. He rides a goat and is married to Swāha.

When Brahma was performing the act of love, Agni appeared by mistake before them and Brahma covered him with a cloth and it became a raging fire. Begged by all those engulfed, Vishnu wiped his forehead and a drop of sweat occupied the universe and cooled off Agni. Since then Agni is always destroyed (put out) by water. Agni was also cursed by a great rishi to become cruel and all consuming. This angered Agni and he retreated so the gods did not get their offerings. When they prayed to Vishnu, he kindly consoled Agni by stating that although he consumes everything, he remains pure. Agni returned from his retreat and began carrying the offerings to the gods. Agni is the vehicle through which offerings go to the gods. This is the reason most Indian ceremonies have the presence of fire.

After continuously consuming offerings, Agni became unhealthy and so went to see Brahma. Brahma advised him to consume the
48

herbal forest Khāndava which was protected by Indra. Everytime Agni tried to consume it, Indra ordered clouds to shower water and destroy Agni. One day Agni met Krishna and Arjuna and explained the problem to them, asking for their help. They replied that they would gladly help him, but they had no weapons to deal with Indra. Agni then gave Chakra (the wheel) to Krishna, and he gave Gāndīva (great bow) to Arjuna and a chariot. Krishna became the charioteer for Arjuna in the great war that followed. With these two weapons, they sealed off the clouds and Agni consumed the Khāndava and became healthy again.

Once when Shiva and Pārvati were in a situation of intimacy and love making, Agni went before them. Agni had been prompted by Indra who wanted to prevent Shiva and Pārvati from having children. Shiva turned away and in that process his sperm fell. Pārvati was furious for being invaded in their privacy and cursed Agni to bear the sperm and a child. That was too much so Agni prayed to Ganga and requsted her to bear the son of Shiva which she tried, but could not and so she threw the fetus in the sawgrass. That child was Kumāraswamy.

Ahalya

Ahalya was created by Brahma. All of the Devas including Indra wanted to marry her because of her great beauty. Brahma decided that whoever made a trip around the earth and returned to him first would have Ahalya. Off they went on their vehicles, chariots, and rides. In the mean time the great rishi Gautama witnessed a cow giving birth to a calf. Gautama circled the cow and then went to Brahma and asked for Ahalya. As circling around a calving cow is equal to circling around the earth, Brahma gave Ahalya to Gautama. All of the Devas were very disappointed. Indra devised a plan to deceive Ahalya and seduce her. He came as a rooster one day and crowed long before it was dawn. Hearing the rooster, Gautama got up and went to the river to carry out his rituals. During that time Indra disguised as Gautama, appeared before Ahalya and seduced her at which time the real Gautama returned because it was not yet dawn and caught Indra in the act. He was angered and cursed Ahalya to become a stone and Indra to wear all over his body the one organ from which he came, namely the vagina. When they both begged for mercy, Gautama rescinded the curses and said the stone will become Ahalya again when touched by Rāma's feet. As for Indra, Gautama said the vaginas all over his body would appear as eyes to others. Indra is also known as Sahasrāksha (thousand-eyed one).

Airāvata

Airāvata was the white elephant upon which Indra rode. Airāvata was born out of the ocean when it was churned by the Devas and the Daityas.

Aja

Aja was a king and the grandfather of Rāma. He was the son of Raghu and he was married to Indumati. Aja's grandfather was Dilipa and his son was Dasaradha who was Rāma's father.

50

Ajāmukhi

Ajāmukhi was the daughter of Surasa and Kasyapa. She often seduced handsome men into romantic relationships. One such relationship was with Dūrvasa with whom she bore Ilvala and Vātapi.

Akshaya

Akshaya was the son of Rāvana and a great warrior. He was killed in a fight with the great Hanumān while Lanka was burning.

Akshayapātra

Akshayapātra was the "never empty pot". When the Pāndavas went into the forest, many brahmins followed them and Yudhistira (Dharmaja) was agonizing about how to feed the entourage. Dhaumya asked Yudhistira to pray to the Sun and the Sun gave him a copper bowl. Whatever was cooked in that bowl became unlimited, thus leading to the saying "one has an Akshayapātra", meaning one has unlimited supplies.

Amba

Amba was the oldest daughter of the king of Kāsi (Benares) and had two sisters, Ambika and Ambālika. The king refused Bhīshma when he asked for the hands of these women in marriage for his half-brothers. Bhīshma fought a minor war and kidnapped the three daughters and took them to Hastināpuram. Amba told Bhīshma that she was in love with prince Sālva so he should let her go, which he did. She went to prince Sālva and explained to him how she was kidnapped and requested Bhīshma to let her go, thus her honor and virginity were untarnished. Sālva did not accept her and totally devastated, she returned to Bhīshma and asked him to marry her.

Bhīshma had taken an oath never to marry and so refused her. Angrily, Amba went into the forest to make tapas to take revenge on Bhīshma. She encountered wise men in the forest who told her that tapas were for rugged men and not for sensitive women such as herself. She should instead request Parasurāma (the guru of Bhīshma) to insist that either Sālva or Bhīshma should accept her. She went to Parasurāma, explained the situation and asked for his help. When Parasurāma asked whom he should insist on, she replied Bhīshma. Parasurāma then approached Bhīshma and Bhīshma performed all the honors accorded a guru and asked what the guru's desire was. When told what it was, namely taking Amba as his wife, he politely refused. This angered Parasurāma, and the two fought a fierce battle. No one was winning and the battle raged on. When all the Devas begged the two to stop because they were wasting their great strength on a cause unworthy of either one, they put an end to the battle. Totally disappointed, Amba went to the forest and prayed to Shiva. Shiva granted her wish to kill Bhīshma in the next life when she would come as both daughter and son of Drupada and slay Bhīshma in the battle. This bisexual child (eunoch) was Shikhandi who appeared in front of Bhīshma in the war and felled him.

Ambālika and Ambika

Ambālika and Ambika were the two sisters of Amba and were married to Chitrāngada and Vichitravīrya, two half-brothers of Bhīshma. They were widowed early in life, but each bore a son through Vyāsa. These sons were Dhrutarāstra (the blind king) and Pāndu (the pale king) whose sons waged the epic battle Mahabhārata.

Anasūya

Anasūya was the daughter of Devahūti and Kardama and the wife of Atri. She was one of the most powerful women (Pativrata) who believed that serving her husband was the greatest thing a wife could do. On one occasion Brahma, Vishnu, and Shiva were riding on their vahanas toward Mount Meru when suddenly they were unable to go any further. Garuda (Vishnu's ride) informed them that this was Atri's ashram and his wife was the great Anasūya and no one could pass over their ashram. All three decided to take alternative routes, but were eager to test the power of

Anasūya. They disguised themselves as Brahmins and came to Atri's ashram. Atri welcomed them and after the appropriate hospitality rituals, offered them dinner. They accepted readily but on the condition that whoever served them should serve them in the nude. That put a bind on Atri and he looked at his wife who agreed to this condition. Brahma, Vishnu, Shiva, and Atri sat at the raised seats and Anasūya came and sprinkled some water and rice. Immediately the three became little children, and Anasūya served them in the nude. She went to retrieve her sari, and came back dressed and sprinkled more water. The three of them became Brahmins again. After the dinner Anasūya converted them into children and kept them in her ashram.

Pārvati, Lakshmi, and Saraswati came searching for their husbands and Anasūya kindly converted them back and gave them to their wives. The three gods were so pleased, they asked Anasūya for any wish. She wished to have children like them and that wish was granted. Those children were Chandra, Dūrvasa, and Dattātreya.

When Kausika was cursed to die at Sunrise his wife, another pativrata, ordered the Sun not to rise. The whole world was in darkness and nothing was functioning so the gods approached Brahma who told them only Anasūya could help. They went and begged Anasūya. She went to the Ashram of Kausika and asked his wife to rescind the order and assured her that she would make her husband come alive. The order was rescinded and the Sun rose and soon after that Anasūya brought Kausika back to life.

Rāma, Lakshmana, and Sīta were also at Atri's ashram during their sojourn in the forest. Anasūya taught all the secrets of pātivratya (serving the husband) and also gave her flowers that would not wilt and a sari that would never become dirty. It was those flowers and that sari which helped Sīta to remain fresh and clean in her captivity.

Angada

Angada was a vānara (monkey) and the son of Vāli and Tara. Rumor had it that Angada was actually the son of Vāli and Mandōdari, but was raised by Tara. After Vāli was killed by Rāma and Sugrīva was installed as king of Kishkindha, Angada was made the crown prince of Kishkindha. Angada helped Rāma search for his wife Sīta, but when he learned that she had been kidnapped by Ravana, he felt his mission had failed. He could not see Sīta and bring the news to Rāma. Instead of going back to Kishkindha unsuccessfully, he decided to end his life by jumping into a fire. At that point Jāmbavanta (Bear King) intervened and said Hanumān would cross the ocean and see Sīta and bring the news that she was still alive. When the war ensued between Rāma and Rāvana, Angada fought on the side of Rāma and killed Mahakāya, the commander of Rāvana's forces. After the war ended and Rāma went to Ayodhya, Sugrīva followed him and Angada became king of Kishkindha.

In a later life, Angada was born as a hunter and killed Krishna by mistake, thus avenging his father Vāli's death.

Angirasa

Angirasa was the son of Brahma and a great rishi. When Agni

went into tapas, Angirasa was installed in his position, and Agni was disappointed when he returned and found out that his position was taken. Angirasa gave Agni his position back and agreed to become his son. His wife was Sivasraddha and one of their sons was Bruhaspati (guru of Devas).

Anjana

Anjana was a vānara maiden. When Vāyu (the God of wind) saw her, he fell in love with her and asked her to make love with him. He also assured her that her virginity would not be forfeited. A son was born out of this relationship whose name was Anjaneya. Anjaneya was also called Hanumān. Hanumān became a great general and helped Rāma conquer Rāvana.

Arjuna

Arjuna was the son of Kunti and Pāndu, actually the son of Kunti and Indra. Kunti had three sons, one with Yama (Yudhistira or Dharmaja), one with Indra (Arjuna), and one with Vāyu (Bhīma), and another one from the Sun (Karna) before she became the wife of Pāndu. Arjuna and Karna were both great warriors, particularly strong in archery. When Pāndu died, his widow Kunti came to Hastinapuram with her sons and her stepsons Nakula and Sahadeva. All of her sons were training in the martial arts and archery under the tutelage of Drōna. Drōna noticed Arunja's talent and favored him over all the others including his own son

Aswatthāma. As one story goes, one day Drōna asked all of his pupils to aim at the eye of a bird and asked them what they saw. Everyone answered that they saw the bird's eye and patches of blue sky and a few trees. When Arjuna was asked what he saw, he replied, "I see only the eye of the bird and nothing else Master". At that utter concentration Drōna was pleased and so Arjuna became his favorite pupil.

After finishing his studies, Arjuna asked Drōna what his wish was as Guru-Dakshina (teacher reward). Drōna said he would like Arjuna to defeat King Drupada and bring him in chains. Arjuna went to war with Drupada, defeated him, and brought him in chains to Drōna. Drōna reminded Drupada of a derogatory statement he made when they were young. Drōna then unchained Drupada and sent him back with due hospitality.

Arjuna, his four brothers, and his mother Kunti were on their way to Varanasi (Benares) disguised as Brahmins. They entered Drupada's city where they saw the challenge of the fish-machine. The man who could shoot the fish in the revolving machine would be married to Drupada's most beautiful daughter Draupadi. Many princes attempted to shoot the fish but failed. Next the Brahmins were given the chance to win Draupadi. Arjuna asked his older brother Dhramaja for permission to participate and easily shot the fish to the amazement of everyone there. They went home and told the good news to their mother Kunti that they had won a prize and brought it home with them. Kunti declared that all five should share it without knowing what the gift was. To keep their mother's order, they all became husbands of Draupadi, thus Draupadi had five husbands. In order to have no disputes about who should have Draupadi at what time, Nārada came and made the rule that starting from Dharmaja each one shall have Draupadi for one year at a time and the cycle would repeat with Dharmaja again.

One day Arjuna was bathing in the Ganga and there a nāga maiden fell in love with him and took him into her palace and forced him to make love to her. He obliged and then went to the city of Manipuram. There he fell in love with princess Chitrāngada and fathered a son Babhruvāhana. He then went to Dvāraka, the city where Krishna was and fell in love with his sister Subhadra and married her. Their child was Abhimanya.

Arjuna and Krishna helped Agni consume the Khāndava forest and as a reward Agni gave Arjuna the great bow Gāndiva and a chariot on which Arjuna would remain undefeated. After the battle was over, Krishna asked Arjuna to step down and look after the weapons. As soon as he stepped down, the chariot caught fire and was consumed along with the weapons. (see Agni)

In Hastinapuram jealousy ran high between the Kauravas and the Pāndavas. Duryodhna, the oldest son of Dhrutarāshtra and head of the Kauravas, challenged Dharmaja to a poker game in which Dharmaja lost all his wealth, jewels, and land. When he announced he had nothing more, Duryodhana remarked that he could bet his wife. Dharmaja lost his wife in the game and at the end Draupadi was dragged to the court and Dussāsana (a brother of Duryodhana) was asked to strip her naked. She pleaded for mercy, but none was shown. She prayed to Krishna to save her honor, and sure enough as one sari was stripped another appeared on her and it only made Dussāsana weary and tired, and he finally gave up. For revenge, Bhīma promised to split Dussāsana's chest and drink his blood, which he did later after felling him in a battle. One of the conditions of the game was that the loser had to spend twelve years in the forests and another year incognito. If during that year they were found and recognized, they would have to repeat the whole cycle again. The Pāndavas packed their few belongings and left for the forests.

Arjuna was carrying out tapas in the forest when Shiva came in the form of a hunter chasing a boar and challenged him to a fight. The two fought fiercely and Shiva was pleased with Arjuna's courage and appeared to him in his own form.   Arjuna immediately prostrated himself before Shiva and Shiva gave him one of the greatest weapons, Pasupata. Indra was so pleased with his son getting such an honor that he took him to his city. There many rishis recognized that Arjuna was none other than the great Nara and so honored him with many gifts. While he was at the court, Urvasi (one of the apsaras) fell in love with him, but Arjuna refused her. Angrily she cursed him that he would lose his manhood for one year. On the way back from the heavens, Arjuna saw Duryodhana shackled by Chitrāswa, so he fought with him and freed Duryodhana. On the way he saw Saindhava trying to assault Draupadi, so he fought and flattened him and saved Draupadi. During the twelve years in the forests, the Pāndavas slowly prepared themselves for the final year of incognito. For that they went to the kingdom of Virāta and posed as common people seeking work. Dharmaja became court counsel, Arjuna became a eunuch teaching dancing for the princess, Bhīma became a cook, Nakula and Sahadeva became horse trainers, and Draupadi became a servant maid. (see Pāndavas)

59

The year was passing and the Kauravas were desperately looking for the Pāndavas. They seized the cow herds of Virāta. Virāta had a son called Uttara who was boasting how easily he could defeat the Kauravas and bring back the herds. He took Arjuna as his charioteer and went to battle the Kauravas. As soon as he saw them and their great strength, he begged Arjuna to turn back and return home. Arjuna said he would help him, if he did not mind going past a cave where he had hidden his bow Gāndiva. He took the Gāndiva and battled the Kauravas and drove them away. Fortunately that was the last day of the incognito year, and they took their true forms and appeared before Virāta to thank him for his help. Virāta was stunned because he never expected to have the great Pāndavas in his employment. He appreciated their help and offered his daughter Uttara in marriage to Arjuna. Arjuna said he was not available, but he would like his son Abhimanya to marry Uttara. A grand wedding was arranged and the couple had a son called Parīkshit. (see Abhimanya)

Since they had completed all the conditions of the lost poker game, the Pāndavas requested Duryodhana to give them their land or at least enough for them to live on independently. Duryodhana refused and said they did not have any claims. After all negotiations failed, there ensued a great battle. On one side there were the armies of the Kauravas and their allies under the command of Bhīshma, and on the other the armies of the Pāndavas and their allies headed by Arjuna. Arjuna took a good look at the enemy and said to Krishna, his charioteer: "Oh Krishna all I see are my relations, friends, and teachers. What do I gain by killing all these men? It saddens me immensely!" At this point

Krishna taught Arjuna the Bhagavadgīta and explained that he was only an instrument and everything was decided long before him. He must be courageous and perform what is expected of him. Thus began the great battle of Kurukshetra.

Bhīshma was the commander of the Kaurava army and fought fiercely destroying many of the Pāndava units. He was ferocious and no one could defeat him. At one point even Krishna was annoyed and angrily wanted to kill Bhīshma by his Chakra. Arjuna begged him not to do this and assured Krishna there would be a way to kill Bhīshma. (see Amba) When the Pāndavas planted Sikhandi, Bhīshma stopped fighting and immediately Arjuna felled him. Bhīshma's command lasted ten days. Drōna then became the commander-in-chief. He too was fighting fiercely and inflicting enormous damages on the Pāndava armies. Drōna was tricked to his death when someone told him that his son was dead. Karna became the next commander-in-chief. Both Bhīshma and Drōna were sympathetic to the Pāndavas, but not Karna. He hated Arjuna and considered him a rival. When Karna became the commander, it meant total destruction for the Pāndavas. On the first day Karna fought and defeated Dharmaja, Bhīma, and Nakula, but he let them go because of a promise he made to Kunti his mother as well as theirs, a fact they did not know until after the war. When Arjuna went to see how brother Dharmaja was doing, Dharmaja asked him if had slain Karna. When he heard it was not the case, he became angry and hurled a few insults at Arjuna. This infuriated Arjuna and he drew his sword. Krishna appeared suddenly and diffused the quarrel. The second day of battle was even fiercer; both Indra and Sun were watching from the heavens while their sons were fighting. Karna

61

used the Nāga-weapon aimed at the throat of Arjuna. Krishna saw this and pressed the chariot with his foot and it was depressed just enough to miss Arjuna's head. The weapon instead swept past Arjuna's crown (kirīta). At this time Karna's curses began to materialize and his chariot sank into the ground and could not be budged. He climbed down and tried to lift the chariot with his shoulder. At that time Krishna urged Arjuna to slay Karna even though he was on the ground and unarmed. The last day Salya took the command and was defeated by Arjuna. The whole battle lasted 18 days, Bhagavadgīta had 18 chapters, Vyāsa wrote 18 Puranas, and it was 18 years since the Pandavas married Draupadi.

When the victory was won, the Pāndavas took the empire and Dhramaja ruled for a very long time with the help of his brother Arjuna. When Dharamaja wanted to perform Aswamēdhayāga (horse sacrifice), Arjuna led the horse to defeat whoever captures it. On the way his son Babhruvāhana heard that his father was coming with the horse, so he went to greet Arjuna. Arjuna insulted him by commenting that a courageous man captures the horse and not greets its defender. This infuriated Babhruvāhana and he fought with Arjuna and caused him to faint. Chtrāngada cried and asked the Nagas to revive Arjuna, which they did.

Arjuna's strength was slowly fading and he wanted to see Krishna. He went to Dvāraka only to find out that both Krishna and Rāma (actually Balarāma) had passed away and all the women and children of Dvāraka were in distress. He performed the necessary rituals and returned to Indraprastha (today this is known as Delhi) and told the news to Dharmaja. At this point Dharmaja was distressed and he made Parīkshit the king and retired to the forests with his brothers and Draupadi. During the trip, one by one Draupadi, then Bhīma, then Nakula, and finally Sahadeva died. Arjuna's Gāndiva was gone and he too fell and died. Only Dharmaja survived to ascend to the heavens.

Arundhati

Arundhati was the daughter of Kardama and Devahāti and the wife of Vasishta. After finishing his studies, Vasishta was trying to find a bride. He took a fist full of sand and asked various women to cook it for him. Most all of the women thought he was crazy except one who lived among the untouchables. She was Arundhati and she took the sand, put it in the pot, and prayed to Shiva. The contents of the pot soon became cooked rice and when she served that to Vasishta, he remarked that he would eat it only when cooked by a married woman. He asked for her hand and her parents readily agreed and she became his wife. He then gave her his Kamandalam (special vessel made of copper with a handle and hook) and asked her to look after it until he returned. She constantly looked at the vessel without distraction. Years went by without a trace of Vasishta. Her gaze was so intense that the world began to feel the heat. Even when Brahma and others asked her to stop, she ignored their requests. They searched and brought Vasishta to her and she turned her sight towards him. She is one of the great Pativratas and became a star next to Vasishta. In a Hindu marriage the couple always ceremoniously looked at the star Arundhati immediately after saying their vows.

Ardhanārīswari

A Gana by the name of Bhrungi prayed to Shiva alone and angered Pārvati because he did not include her in the prayer. She dried him and he was left as pulp when Shiva appeared and gave him a stick to hold. Pārvati felt belittled and angrily went to Kedāreswara and there Gautama explained to her the truth and she prayed to Shiva. When Shiva appeared, she became half of him again. The meaning of Ardhanārīswari is half-human half-goddess.

Aryama

Aryama was the son of Kasyapa and Aditi. He was also one of the twelve Suns.

Aswani

Aswani was the daughter of Daksha and Dharani (Earth) and the wife of Chandra.

Aswatthāma

Aswatthāma was the son of Drōna and Krupi. When he was a baby, Aswatthāma cried loudly like the great horse Uchaisrava and was thus named Aswatthāma. As a child and young adult, he learned all of the martial arts from his father along with the Kauravas and the Pāndavas. His special talent was that he could use his bow in the dark. Drōna gave him an excellent weapon Brahmasirāstra, which could destroy anyone. Once when he was visiting Krishna, he asked Krishna to trade this weapon with his Chakra. Krishna asked him why he wanted to trade and he replied by saying that he did not want to be defeated by anyone. Krishna told him even his best friend Arjuna never asked for this Chakra, but since Aswatthāma came as a guest and asked specifically, Krishna offered to let him take any weapon in his arsenal, but whatever he touched first would be what he had to pick up and take with him. When all the weapons were in front of him, Aswatthāma touched the Chakra but could not lift it. In the Great War between the Kauravas and the Pāndvas, he was neutral until his father was killed by cheating and Duryodhana was felled by Bhīma by hitting below the belt. He consoled Duryodhana and said he would do something to please him in his last moments. He set out to kill the Pāndavas in the night when they were sleeping. He justified this sort of action for himself, because the Pāndavas had killed Bhīshma, his father Drōna, Karna, and Duryodhana all by cheating. On the way he met Shiva and not knowing who he was, began to shoot arrows at him. Shiva simply swallowed them, and at that moment, Aswatthāma knelt before Shiva and asked for forgiveness. Shiva was pleased and presented him with a sword. Aswatthāma then entered the chamber where the children of the Pāndavas were sleeping and cut their heads off and took them to show to Duryodhana. Draupadi heard this news and cried before Bhīma and asked for revenge. Bhīma captured Aswatthāma and brought him before Draupadi. She took pity on him and asked Bhīma to spare his life but remove the special jewel in his head. As a curse the wound did not heal and Aswatthāma was to spend

65

three millennia on earth stinking because of his wound. *(Some Indians believe he is in the Himalayas and profess to have seen him as a red/flaxen haired big man roaming the slopes. Could this be the Yeti?)*

Aswini(s)

The Aswinis were the sons of Sun and Sangya. Sangya could not stand the bright Sun and so went north into the hills. Sun disguised himself as a horse and went to visit Sangya. She recognized him and loved him in that form. They had two children and these were Aswinis. One was called Nasatya and the other Dasru. They were unequaled in medicine and became physicians for the Devas. They fixed limbs for those who lost them in wars and artificially inseminated women. They presented a child to Vadhrimati whose husband was a eunuch. They rescued and revived several drowning victims. They also revived the vision of a shepherd who killed goats to feed them and was cursed with blindness. Once they saw a young beautiful woman named Sukanya bathing naked in a lake. They approached her and asked her to come to them instead of her old husband Chyavana. She told her husband what these two young men said, and Chyavana proposed that all three of them should become identical and then whomever she chose, he could keep her. All three became young men with glistening bodies and muscular limbs, yet Sukanya somehow chose Chyavana. Chyavana became young again and a friend of Aswinis.

Atiradha

Atiradha was a charioteer and friend of Dhrutarāstra. He saw the basket in which Karna slept floating in the river. Atiradha took him home and raised him as his own son. His wife was Rādha and they had no other children.

Atri

Atri was a rishi and the son of Brahma. Anasūya was his wife. When he prayed for children Brahma, Vishnu, and Shiva appeared to him and all three blessed him with sons. Brahma's son was Chandra, Vishnu's was Dattātreya, and Shiva's was Dūrvāsa. (see Anasūya)

Aurva

Aurva was a rishi from the Bhrugu family and the son of Chyavana. The royal family of Krutavīrya was torturing the Bhrugu family for monies, cattle, and wealth. They also tried to kill Chyavana's pregnant wife and her child. She hid the child in her thigh (Uru in Sanskrit) and thus he was born Aurva. Upon seeing the child, the Krutavīryas became blind and begged her for sight. She said they became blind not by her but by her son Aurva. They prayed to Aurva and got their sight back, but suddenly in a rage killed many of the Bhrugu family members. At that point, Aurva became angry and began great tapas to burn the three worlds (the level one, the one above and the one below). His ancestors then appeared before him and explained why they were killed like that. It was staged killing only, because if they were to commit suicide (in order to leave the earth), they would not have access to the heavens. They staged it to happen this way and asked Aurva to cancel his tapas. Aurva agreed to this but the tapas had gone too far and had resulted in a fire that could only be contained by the sea. The fire took the form of a horse and entered the sea. Aurva had a son Ruchika and a daughter Ayōnija who became wife of Dūrvāsa.

Babhruvāhana

Babhruvāhana was the son of Arjuna and Chitrāngada. He lived in Manipura and had not seen his father for a long time. When Arjuna was leading the horse for their Aswamēdha Yagna, Babhruvāhana went to meet his father and greet him. Arjuna was angry that one of his caste was a coward and chided him for not fighting. At the same time Ulūchi, who was from the land of Nagas (snakes), saw Babhruvāhana and exhorted him to fight Arjuna. During the confrontation both fell and became unconscious. Chitrāngada begged Ulūchi to revive them, which he did. (see Arjuna)

Badari

Badari was a forest in the foothills of the Himalayas where many rishis including Nara and Nārāyana established their ashrams and meditated.

Baka

Baka was a demon torturing the people of Ekachakrapura. He finally agreed to leave them alone if they would provide him with a daily cart full of food, two buffaloes, and a man for him to eat. When the Pāndavas agreed to this arrangement, Bhīma volunteered to take the cart with food and give it to Baka. Instead Bhīma began to eat the food himself. Baka was angry and hit Bhīma with his fists. A fight ensued in which Bhīma killed Baka. He returned to the village and announced the news of Baka's demise. The villagers were happy and thanked Bhīma.

Baka (2)

Baka was a disciple of Shiva. One day he picked lotus flowers from a lake that belonged to Pārvati. Guards of the lake arrested him and took him to Pārvati. Pārvati was angry because she had reserved the flowers for a special offering to Krishna and so cursed Baka to become a demon on earth. She also declared that he would be redeemed by Krishna. Baka, living his days as a demon, encountered Krishna one day and swallowed him. Krishna tore his throat open and emerged, killing Baka in the process. Baka then resumed his previous form and went back to heaven.

Balarāma

Balarāma was the son of Rohini and Vasudeva and the half-brother of Krishna. When Vishnu was incarnated as Krishna, Adisesha became the seventh fetus of Devaki. Devaki's brother Kamsa was determined to kill all of Devaki's fetuses. The seventh one was taken and implanted in Rohini's womb and thus Adisesha

69

was born as Balarāma. He had four brothers besides Krishna, Gada, Sarana, Durmada, and Vipula. He was also known as Sankarshana. Balarāma was the great guru of gada (club) warfare and taught both Bhīma and Duryodhana in the martial arts. Just as Drōna was slightly biased in favor of Arjuna, Balarāma was biased in favor of Duryodhana. He was not in favor of his sister Subhadra marrying Arjuna. Krishna engineered a trick to marry Arjuna and Subhadra. Arjuna came disguised as a hermit and Balarāma showed his hospitality by ordering Subhadra to serve him. Subhadra fell in love with Arjuna and they were married when Balarāma was away. When Devaki wished to see her dead children, both Krishna and Balarāma went to the netherworld and brought Devaki's children back to show her.

Balarāma married Revati and when Krishna married Rukmini, her brother Rukmi was against the marriage. Rukmi wanted Rukmini to marry Sisupāla and he fought Krishna and was defeated. Balarāma asked Krishna not to kill Rukmi, but shave his head and send him back. When Rukmi was hurling insults at Krishna and Rāma, he was slain by Balarāma. He became angry at the city of Hastinapuram and so battered the city with his club. Balarāma went to the river Yamuna with his gopika friends and called Yamuna. When she did not respond, he took his club and threatened to crush Yamuna. Yamuna then appeared as a woman and prayed to Balarāma. Just as Krishna was siding with the Pāndavas, Balarāma was sympathetic towards the Kauravas. He wanted his daughter Shasirekha to marry Duryodhana's son Lakshmana, but it did not happen. Balarāma attended the marriage of Abhimanya and asked the Pāndavas to send a message to the Kauravas not to go to war. When the message failed, he did not wish to take sides in the Great War so he went on a pilgrimage until the war was over. On one of his pilgrimages, he entered the ashram of Naimisha. All the rishis stood up on seeing Balarāma except Sūta who was bent on insulting him. He took a darbha (a saw grass blade) and hit him saying unworthy people become arrogant with power and Sūta died. When the rishis prayed to him for forgiveness, he brought Sūta back to life, which made him respectful of others.

Towards the end of the war, Balarāma heard of the fight between Bhīma and Duryodhana and came to Kurukshetra to prevent that fight, but was too late and it took place anyway. When he saw Bhīma hitting Duryodhana on the thigh (below the belt), he was angry and lifted his club to kill Bhīma. Krishna intervened and diffused the feelings of anger. Balarāma left Dvāraka (their city) and left his physical body in a forest. Arjuna and Krishna were searching for him and found the dead body. Arjuna performed the proper rituals for Balarāma. The name Ramakrishna comes from the inseparable Balarāma and Krishna.

Bali

Bali was the son of Virochana and grandson of Prahlāda. He was thus the great grandson of Hiranyakasipa. Bali was married to Ashana and had a daughter called Ratnamāla and four sons Bāna, Dhrutarāshtra, Nikumbhanābha, and Vibhīshana. Bali was a very good king, he always told the truth and was a great giver never telling his people "no". There was a great rift between the Devas and the Danavas. Bali was the king of the Danavas and his people were suffering greatly and unjustly at the hands of the Devas. He consulted his guru, Sukrācharya and on his advice made great tapas and acquired enormous powers. Bali was not about to waste them on any small cause, so he declared war on Indra, lord of the heavens. Indra consulted his guru, Bruhaspati and was advised to leave gracefully because at that time Bali could not be conquered by any one except Vishnu or Shiva. Ages passed and Indra prayed to Vishnu. Vishnu said that Bali was such a righteous king that only some form of trickery could weaken him. He also said he would incarnate as a dwarf Brahmin and conquer Bali. Vishnu entered the womb of Aditi (Kasyapa's wife) and was born as Vāmana (means small fellow). He mastered all of the Vedas and associated knowledge as a little boy and performed the thread ceremony as a Brahmin boy. Soon Vāmana set out to see Bali. Bali met him and did all the rituals a Brahmin deserves and asked what his wish was. The boy Brahmin replied all he needed was three feet of space. At that point Bali's guru intervened and cautioned Bali that this little Brahmin boy was none other than Vishnu and he was going to destroy him. He should thus withdraw his offer. Bali refused the warning and approved the request of Vāmana by pouring water from his kalasa (pot). When no water came because Bali's guru blocked the opening, Vāmana took a darbha (reed) and poked through the spout and pierced through the eye of Sukrācharya. The guru of the Danavas became one-eyed. Then the little Vāmana occupied the whole earth with one foot, the sky and the other worlds with another, and asked where can he put his third foot. Bali looked at him and said: "my body is still mine, so please put your foot on my head". Vāmana put his foot on Bali's head and crushed him. At that point Prahlāda appeared and begged Vāmana to spare Bali because he did not deserve that sort of punishment. Vāmana made Bali the king of the netherworld and became his gatekeeper to honor him.

Rāvana heard of this trickery and wanted to avenge the Danavas. He went to the netherworld and asked Bali where Vishnu was so he could fight him. Bali pointed to the first gate and said that the keeper of the first gate was Vishnu. A surprised Rāvana showed his respect to Bali and left.

When Devaki wished to see her dead children, Balarāma and Krishna came to Bali for help. Bali gladly obliged and they showed Devaki her children from the netherworld.

Bali (2)

Bali was the son of king Sutav. One day when he was bathing in the Ganga, he saw someone chanting Vedas and floating by. He quickly recognized that someone as rishi Dīrghatama, rescued him, and took him home. Since Bali had no children, he ordered his wife Sudheshna to have children by Dīrghatama. Sudheshna did not like the appearance of this old man so she sent her servant instead. The servant had two sons and Bali was happy thinking they were his sons. Dīrghatama said they were not Sudheshna's, only the servant's. He begged Dīrghatama and ordered Sudheshna again to mate with the rishi. She did and bore a very strong, valorous, and powerful son named Anga who ruled the kingdom for a long time. He had four sons Vanga, Kalinga, Simha, and Andhra. They established the four states of Bengal, Orissa, Bihar, and Andhra.

Basavanna

Basavanna was the son of Madiraju and Madamamba. They had no children, so Madamamba prayed to Nandi and became pregnant. After a three-year pregnancy, she still had not delivered. She prayed to Shiva and Nandi appeared in her dream and told her that he would be born as her male child and she should name him Basavanna. Basavanna was born and when his father tried to perform Upanayanam (thread ceremony), the boy objected to it and left home. He married his first cousin and visited Shiva's temple and stayed there praying to Shiva. Shiva appeared and gave him enlightenment. A king called Bijjala asked him to become his minister, which he did. Once Shiva appeared as a guest and asked him for food. Basavanna recognized the guest as Shiva himself and said there was very little that he could give to Shiva except prayer. Shiva was very satisfied and blessed Basavanna.

Once a mendicant came and asked for all the money in the safe. Basavanna gave it to him and the others saw the act and told the king. The king was angry and asked Basavanna why he had taken money that did not belong to him. Basavanna said he did not need any money and he would ask the king if he did. The king ordered the safe to be brought into the court and opened. Lo and behold, all the money was in it and nothing was missing. The mendicant was Shiva himself.

Bhagadatta

Bhagadatta was the son of Narakāsura. He was very fond of the Pāndavas, but on one occasion he was involved in a fight with Arjuna and the fight went on for several days and ended in a draw at the urging of Indra. In the Great War however, Bhagadatta fought on the side of the Kauravas. His father Naraka gave him a powerful weapon, Vaishnavāstra, which he used against Arjuna in the battle. Since the weapon could not be neutralized by anyone except Vishnu, his incarnation Krishna prevented it from killing Arjuna. After this weapon failed, Bhagadatta was weakened and Arjuna killed him with his weaponry.

Bhagīratha

Bhagīratha was the grandson of Sagara. When all of Sagara's sons (sixty thousand) were killed and their souls were unable to go to heaven, Sagara prayed to Vishnu. Vishnu granted him a boon and when he asked for an offspring that would redeem his sons, Vishnu asked all of Sagara's sons' wives to pour their menstrual blood into a specially made pot. Out of that pot, a child was born and that was Bhagīratha. As there was no semen involved, Bhagīratha was weak and could not get up and down. One day a rishi was passing by and Bhagīratha was trying to pay his respects by getting up but could not. The rishi was angry because he thought Bhagīratha was insulting him and cursed him conditionally by stating that if he was really insulting him he should become ashes, but if he was not, then he should become a strong and handsome man. Bhagīratha thus became a strong prince. His grandfather told him how his fathers were all destroyed by a curse of Kapila, and the only way they could go to heaven was by bringing Ganga to earth and making her flow over their ashes. He prayed to Ganga first and when Ganga agreed to come down but said the earth could not stand her impact, he prayed to Shiva. Shiva agreed to catch Ganga in his hair and slowly let her down. When that happened, Ganga was flowing zigzag with waves and tides, but her path had angered Jahna who quickly swallowed Ganga. Bhagīratha then prayed to him and Ganga was released from his ear. Ganga absorbed the ashes of Sagara's sons and they all went to heaven. Ganga is also called Bhāgīrahti and any project that requires great effort to complete is referred to as a Bhagīratha project.

When Agastya drank all the oceans, they were filled by Ganga to keep the ocean worlds alive. (see Agastya)

Bharadwāja

Bharadwāja was the son of Bruhaspati. Bruhaspati fell in love with his brother's pregnant wife Mamata and raped her. Mamata could not bear both fetuses in her womb so she discarded Bruhaspati's fetus. This fetus became a son, Bharadwāja and he was one of the seven Rishis. Bharata, who was childless, adopted Bharadwāja as his son. One day Bharadwāja was meditating on the banks of the Ganga when he saw Ghrutāchi who was a heavenly socialite and one of the apsaras, and fell in love with her and experienced ejaculation. He kept the semen in a box and from that Drōna was born.

Bharata

Bharata was the son of Dushyantha and Sakuntala. When Sakuntala was pregnant with Bharata, she lived in the ashram of Kanva. Bharata learned all of the skills and knowledge of the rishis. As a boy and young man he was able to tame and control wild animals. He was also called Sarvadamana meaning "all tamer". When he grew up, Kanva asked Sakuntala to go to Dushyanta and introduce his son to him. When she went to the court of Dushyanta, he refused to recognize her and then a voice from the heaven (Akasavani) pronounced that the boy really was his. He further said that Sakuntala was absolutely faithful to him, and he should bear responsibility for them. Bharata whose name means bearer of responsibility succeeded his father to the throne and reigned for a long time peacefully.

Although Bharata had three wives he was childless. His wives were destroying his children thinking they would never be as great as their father. When he prayed the rishis brought Bharadwāja and asked Bharata to adopt him.

Bharata (2)

Bharata was the son of Rushabha and Jayanti. He married princess Panchajanani and had five children. After Rushabha, Bharata became king and established a great kingdom in what is north India today, and because of him it was called Bharatavarsha. He had seven brothers who ruled parts of Bharatavarsha as his deputies. After reigning several years,

Bharata transferred the kingdom to his sons and went into the forest for tapas. There he saw a deer calfing and in that process the mother died. He took pity on the deer fawn *[bambi]* and took her to his ashram. When he died he was born as a deer in the next life, but had knowledge of his previous life. After life as a deer, he was born as a son of Brahmin Angirasa and was disliked by his half-brothers. They set him up as a sacrifice to Kali and at the moment of sacrifice, Kali appeared and slew the others. Bharata then went on a walking tour of the country where the king of Sindh was going with a big entourage to see the great Kapila and learn the ultimate truth from him. Someone in the entourage was tired and put his burden on Bharata who carried on and didn't say anything. When the king became angry because his belongings were being carried by someone unknown to him, Bharata advised him that anger, cursing, and vanity belong to the body and not the soul. After all he was going to Kapila for enlightenment. The king immediately realized that this was not an ordinary man and begged Bharata to enlighten him, which he did. After three lives, Bharata attained Moksha (eternal bliss).

Bharata (3)

Bharata (3) was the son of Dasaratha and Kaika and half-brother of Rāma. When Rāma was about to be crowned, Kaika reminded Dasaratha of a promise he made to her and asked that it be honored. As a condition, she wanted Rāma to go to the forest for twelve years and her son Bharata should become the king. This broke the heart of Dasaratha and he died, because he so wanted Rāma to be king. At that time Bharata was not even in the palace, he was visiting his uncle and when he returned and heard the news, he was so angry he was about to kill his own mother. He remained composed, and set out to seek Rāma and offer him the throne. On the way he had to cross Ganga and the ferry pilot refused him. He thought Bharata was going to kill Rāma. When Bharata explained why he was going to see Rāma, he was convinced and ferried him to the other side. Bharata approached Chitrakūta, saw Rāma, and prostrated himself in front of him. Bharata begged him loudly to come home, occupy the throne, and reign. Rāma said to him it was his father's wish and they should not dishonor it. Bharata asked Rāma to give him his sandals to be placed on the throne in lieu of Rāma and he would rule until the last day of his exile. If Rāma did not return, he would commit suicide. He ruled Ayodhya in the name of Rāma until he returned.

Bharata (4)

Bharata was a rishi who created the art of dancing and wrote music. Bhrata Nātya is named after him.

Bhētāla

Bhētāla was the lord of ghosts and the king of funeral sites. In a previous life he was Pushpadanta, king of Yugandha. He was a devout worshiper of Shiva. When Shiva appeared before him and asked for his wishes, he wished that Shiva and Pārvati would appear before him every day. The wish was granted and he was seeing Shiva and Pārvati everyday. One day Pārvati requested Shiva to tell her a story, a secret story that only they would know. Pushpadanta overheard the story and when he went to his palace,

79

his wife accused him of betraying her. He explained that he was only seeing Shiva and Pārvati and to prove that point he told her the story Shiva told Pārvati. When Shiva and Pārvati knew of this, they became angry and cursed Pushpadanta to become Bhētāla and made him lord of ghosts and king of funeral sites.

Bhīma

Bhīma was the son of Kunti by Vāyu (God of Wind). When he was ten days old, Kunti took him to a temple. On her journey, Kunti was attacked by a tiger and dropped Bhīma. He fell on a rock and Pāndu came and lifted Bhīma up to see how badly he was hurt. The rock was crushed yet Bhīma was not hurt. After Pāndu's death, Kunti took her children to Hastinapuram. They played with their cousins, Dhrutarāshtra's sons and were very happy. Bhīma never thought of others as evil even though his cousins were jealous of him and also of Arjuna. Bhīma always obeyed his elder brother Dharmaja's orders and never contradicted him. Once when he was keeping watch at night, Hidimbi, a rākshasa woman, came to him and expressed her love for him. Bhīma refused her and his rejection hurt her deeply. She complained to her brother Hidimba who challenged Bhīma to a fight. Bhīma fought with him and killed Hidimba. Dharmaja saw Hidimbi crying, and took pity on her and asked Bhīma to satisfy her. Bhīma agreed and made love to her and they had a son called Ghatotkacha who later aided the Pāndavas in the war. The Pāndavas disguised as Brahmins, entered Ekachakrapuram where Bhīma agreed to drive the food cart to Baka and killed him. (see Baka) After this they went to Drupada's city and Arjuna won the contest for Draupadi.

From there, the Pāndavas went to Indraprasta where they were crowned as princes. Bhīma assisted Dharmaja in his duties as king and once when they were about to perform Rajasuya fest, they faced the mighty Jarāsandha. They disguised themselves as

81

Brahmins to enter his city and challenged him to a fight. He agreed to fight Bhīma and was killed by Bhīma. The Kauravas, especially Duryodhana, were very jealous of them and a poker game was arranged. In that game Dharmaja lost everything. As a condition of the loss, the Pāndavas had to go to the forest for twelve years and then spend one-year incognito. They all went to the forest. One day in the forest, Draupadi saw a lotus flower and thought she would like more. Bhīma went searching and on the way he saw the monkey God Hanumān blocking the way. He asked Hanumān to get out of his way and Hanumān wanted to teach Bhīma a lesson. He said to him that he was an old monkey and he should lift his tail and go on his way. Bhīma thought what a silly idea it was, and tried to lift the tail with his left hand first, and soon with all his strength; but could not. Then he recognized that the old monkey was not any ordinary monkey and so respectfully bowed to Hanumān. Hanumān was also son of Vāyu and thus Bhīma's half-brother.

One day Bhīma went hunting and was wrapped up by a snake. He tried desperately to free himself, but was unable to do so. The snake was none other than Nahusha, a great Brahmin who also ruled the heavens before he was cursed to become a snake. When Bhīma realized this was no ordinary snake, he paid respects and learned from Nahusha some truths about life and existence. At the end of their time in the forest, the Pāndavas went to Virāta to look for jobs so as to remain incognito. Bhīma went as a cook and became chef of the royal household. He was performing several strange feats of strength and pleasing the audiences. Virāta had a brother-in-law called Kīchaka who was harassing Draupadi. Bhīma heard of this and was about to kill him but Dharmaja (whose name was Kankabhat at that time) asked him not to

82

because it would reveal their identity. Bhīma thought of a plan and asked Draupadi to let Kīchaka know that she would wait for him at a certain place and time. When Kīchaka came, it was Bhīma dressed as a woman instead of Draupadi who hugged Kīchaka so strongly that he was crushed to death.

When the year of incognito was over, Bhīma did not participate in the negotiations. He wished there would be no war, but war was to take place and Bhīma fought many of his foes among the Kauravas. He fought with Dussāsana who insulted Draupadi, split his chest and plucked his heart out to present it to Draupadi. After the deaths of Karna and Salya, Duryodhana was hiding under a lake. The Pāndavas challenged him to a fight and as he chose to fight with Bhīma, the great Gada fight ensued. In that fight Bhīma hit him on the thigh (below the belt) at a hint by Krishna. After felling him, he kicked Duryodhana's head with his left foot to insult him. Then they all went to see their uncle Dhrutarāshtra who wanted to hug them to show his affection. When Bhīma's turn came Krishna pulled Bhīma to the side and slipped a steel statue in his place. As Dhrutarāshtra was blind, he hugged the statue and pulverized it to show his anger at Bhīma for killing his son. This would have been the fate of Bhīma had it been him instead of the statue.

After reigning for some time, the news of Krishna's death reached the Pāndavas. They were all saddened and installed Parīkshit as king and abdicated themselves. Sorrowfully they all went to the Himalayas and on the way all of them perished except Dharmaja. Bhīma was second to die.

83

Bhīshma

Bhīshma was the eighth son of Santana and Ganga. When Santana married Ganga, he promised to give his children to Ganga as soon as they were born and Ganga would drown them immediately. In the case of Bhīshma, Santana refused to give him to Ganga and so she left him. Bhīshma grew to be a magnificent man learning the Sastras from Vasishta, martial arts from Parasurāma, and principles from Bruhaspati. He was thus ready to be the king after Santana. One day Santana saw Satyavati, the daughter of Dāsaraj, and fell in love with her. Santana was filled with grief when Dāsaraj refused his request. Bhīshma found the reason and went to Dāsaraj and asked what would it take for him to agree to give Satyavati to his father. Dāsaraj asked that Satyavati's children become kings and Bhīshma agreed immediately, but Dāsaraj was a tough negotiator. He asked what would be the fate of his grandchildren if Bhīshma's children were to be there and protest for their rights. Without blinking an eye, Bhīshma promised he would remain a bachelor so that problem would never arise. Dāsaraj was happy and gave Satyavati to Santana. When Santana heard of this, he realized the sacrifice Bhīshma made to please him and granted him a great gift of Death-as-Desired (Swachhanda Maranam). Bhīshma could not be killed; he dies only of his own wish.

Satyavati bore Santana two children, they were Chitrāngada and Vichitravīrya. Santana died when they were young. When they grew up they were acceptable young men, but were not considered of true royal blood. When the daughters of the monarch of Kashi became eligible for suitable royal men, both

84

Chitrāngada and Vichitravīrya were bypassed as they were not of true royal heritage. This infuriated Bhīshma and he went to Kashi and defeated all the opponents and captured the three daughters of Kashiraja. They were Amba, Ambika, and Ambālika and of these three, Amba refused to accept Bhīshma's brothers. She said she was in love with another prince and so could not love his brothers. Bhīshma let her go and married the other two to his half brothers. Amba went to her lover Sālva only to be ridiculed and refused by him. She came back to Bhīshma and asked him to marry her, but without success. She later would come as Sikhandi and help kill Bhīshma. (see Amba) Bhīshma's half-brothers were not good kings; they picked fights with the Gandharvas and were slain. They died without heirs. Satyavati consulted Bhīshma and urged him to marry someone and produce heirs to the kingdom. Bhīshma said no, a promise was a promise to him and he could not go back on his word. Satyavati said she had another son Vyāsa from Parāsara and he would come to help her. She called him and he appeared and asked what he could do. Satyavati ordered him to produce heirs to the kingdom through Ambika and Ambālika. He agreed and when he mated with Ambika, she was afraid and closed her eyes, so a son was born blind. He was Dhrutarāshtra. When he mated with Ambālika, she too was afraid and held her breath, and a son was born pale and weak. He was Pāndu. Satyavati asked Vyāsa to mate with the servant woman, and from her was born a strong and wise son. He was Vidura. Bhīshma arranged for their education and training and when they grew up, he married them off; Dhrutarāshtra to Gāndhāri and Pāndu to Kunti and Mādri. Dhrutarāshtra and Gāndhāri had one hundred sons and Duryodhana was the oldest. Pāndu had five sons, three from Kunti and two from Mādri.

85

Bhīshma, as the great uncle saw to it that they were all well educated, trained, and prepared for the duties that were to be theirs as rulers of the kingdom. He saw the jealousies growing among Dhrutarāshtra's sons, the Kauravas at the success of the Pāndvas. He persuaded Dhrutarāshtra to give half of the kingdom to Dharmaja. Dharmaja lost all of it gambling to Duryodhana and the Pāndavas had to go to the forest for twelve years and then one year unrecognized. Bhīshma did not like this, but he could not override Duryodhana the king. Finally when it came to war, Bhīshma fought on the side of Duryodhana. He was the first commander of all the Kaurava armies and fought loyally. He also had an ongoing disagreement with Karna. At one point he classified Karna as Ardharatha (half a charioteer) whereas Karna was perhaps at least equal if not better than Bhīshma himself. They both were pupils of the same guru Parasurāma. Angrily Karna refused to fight as long as Bhīshma was on the field. Bhīshma fought relentlessly for ten days and the Pāndavas were completely demoralized under his attacks. They didn't know what to do. At one point even Krishna became angry and threatened to use his Chakra on Bhīshma to kill him. Arjuna begged Krishna not to do that. Finally Dharmaja approached Bhīshma and touched his feet in reverence, and asked how to defeat him. Bhīshma told him that he would not fight with a woman, so if they could find such a person and install her in front of him, he would not fight or fight with closed eyes. They found Sikhandi who was a eunuch and installed her on the chariot. Sikhandi was none other than Amba in a previous life and she was determined to take revenge on Bhīshma (see Amba). Fighting erratically because he could not see to aim, Bhīshma became very susceptible and Arjuna quickly felled him with his arrows. Arjuna then prepared a bed of arrows for Bhīshma to lie down on as

86

Ampasayya visited him. Bhīshma asked for some water, and Arjuna sent an arrow into the ground and out came a fountain of water just like Ganga water. Because of his boon from his father, Bhīshma could choose to die when he pleased and as he was lying there, all the Pānadavs and Kauravas came to pay homage and pleased him, even Karna came and they reconciled. Krishna took away his pain. This was during the cancer equinox and it was not a good time to die. Bhīshma waited until the winter equinox and died on the eleventh day after the first new moon in January. He left this world for the heavens where he really belonged. This day is known as Bhīshma-Ekādasi and as respect to the great man, people fast on that day.

Brahma

Brahma was the son of Vishnu and the creator of the universe. The Brahmahood was a title just like the position of Indra. There were nine Brahmas: Bhrugu, Pulastya, Pulaha, Angirasa, Atri, Kratuvu, Daksha, Vasishta, and Marichi. Brahma was born from the navel of Vishnu. When Vishnu was resting after the great flood, Brahma entered Vishnu's body and saw the universe in him, which he would replicate. Vishnu then closed his nine orifices (navarandhras) and Brahma came out from his navel and became the son of Vishnu. Originally Brahma had five faces, one of which was cut off by Bhairava. This face had the appearance of a donkey. Brahma and Vishnu were arguing about who was greater between them. A lingam appeared between them and whoever found the beginning and the end of the lingam, he was greater. Brahma took off as a swan and Vishnu as a pig. Whoever comes out first he is greater. Brahma saw a flower on a great pillar but couldn't reach it. He decided to lie that he reached the pillar and asked the flower to be his witness. When he said he saw the beginning and the end of the lingam, Vishnu bowed to him with respect. Out of the lingam came Shiva and said Brahma lied and so that face became a donkey's face. Brahma was also cursed to not be worshipped in any temple. Therefore there is no Brahma temple or shrine. When the donkey face was cut off by Bhairava, it stuck to his hand and he had to perform a great ritual to get rid of the skull. Where the skull fell off, that is known as Brahmatīrtha and it has the shape of a skull Brahma-Kapala.

Brahma created Saraswati and married her. He rode on a swan. From his face came the Brahmins, from his arms came Kshatriyas, from his rear came Vaisyas, and from his feet came the Sudras. Brahma first created Sanaka, Sanandana, and Sanatkumara and asked them to expand the world. They refused and Brahma became angry and that became Rudra born from between the eyes of Brahma. This Rudra took eleven forms giving the world eleven Rudras.

Nārada was born from the thigh of Brahma and when he too refused to expand the world, Brahma cursed him to be born as a Sudra lusting for women. This angered Nārada, and he cursed

Brahma that he would not be worshipped.

He then created the nine Brahmas and they in turn agreed to expand the creator's work. When Tripuras (three cities) were destroyed, Brahma became the chariot driver for Shiva who destroyed the Tripuras.

Brahma-Hatya

Brahma-Hatya is the sin of killing a Brahmin. Indra first committed this sin by slaying Vrutra. He begged Brahma to purify him of this sin.

Brahmaputra

Brahmaputra means a river born of Brahma, literally Brahma's son. Brahma fell in love with Amogha, wife of Santanu and approached her when Santanu was not home. Amogha closed the door and threatened to curse Brahma if he did not leave. Brahma could not control his emotion, and masturbated before leaving. When Santanu came home he saw the footprints of a swan and the drops of semen and asked Amogha what happened. When he heard the story, Santanu preserved the sperm for the good of the world, and put it in Amogha. When that child was born, he took the child to the mountains (the Himalayas). The child grew and became the river Brahmaputra. Parasurāma bathed in Brahmaputra to purify himself of the sin of slaying his own mother.

Bruhadradha

Bruhadradha was the king of Magadha and father of Jarāasnadha. (see Jarāsandha)

Bruhaspati

Bruhaspati was the guru of the Devas and the son of Angirasa. Together with Indra, he went to see Shiva. They both disguised themselves as Brahmins and approached Kailas. Shiva wanted to test these two and blocked their path in the form of a naked man. Indra asked him to get out of their way and when Shiva refused, he lifted his Vajrayudha to kill Shiva, and was burnt to ashes. Bruhaspati soon realized who the naked man was and bowed to him respectfully and begged him to revive Indra.

Bruhaspati was married to Tara. Tara was in love with Chandra and had a son by him, Budha. There ensued a great argument between Bruhaspati and Chandra about who the father was. In order to take advantage of the situation, the Asuras (Daityas) sided with Chandra and the Devas sided with Bruhaspati. Fights ensued and Angirasa went to Brahma and asked him to resolve the matter. Brahma came and asked Tara whose son Budha was. When Tara told the truth, Brahma gave Tara to Bruhaspati and Budha to Chandra.

Bruhaspati fell in love with his sister-in-law and raped her even though she was pregnant. The result was a son called Bharadwāja. (see Bhradwāja)

91

Budha

Budha was the son of Tara and Chandra. (see Bruhaspati) He was raised by Chandra's wife Rohini. Sudyumna, a son of Manu, took a swim in a forbidden lake and became a woman. When Budha saw her, he fell in love with her and asked her to follow him to his house. She did and he took her as his wife and they had a son called Purūrava. Budha himself became a Graha and a day in the middle of the week was named after him (Wednesday is known as Budhaday).

Chandra

Chandra was the son of Atri born from his right eye. Chandra went to study under Bruhaspati and fell in love with his wife Tara. A son was born out of their affair. (see Budha) Chandra married Rohini, one of Daksha's daughters. He also married twenty-six other daughters of Daksha. His affections though, were only for Rohini and so the other daughters complained to Daksha. Daksha became very angry and cursed him to diminish and disappear. Afraid of Daksha's curse, Chandra went to Shiva and prayed to him. Shiva promised to protect him and so ensued a great quarrel between Shiva and Daksha. Vishnu came in time and diffused the quarrel and divided Chandra into two halves and gave one to Shiva and the other to Daksha and his daughters who watched him disappear and reappear.

Angered at Daksha's curse, Chandra counter-cursed Daksha and disappeared. There were no crops, medical plants, or medicine and the world was seething with unpleasantness. All of the Devas went to Brahma and prayed to him to find Chandra. Brahma found Chandra in the oceans and advised all of the Devas and Asuras to churn the oceans and Chandra would come out.

One day Ganesha was going to see his parents Shiva and Pārvati after a good meal. Ganesha had a heavy stomach and was walking slowly. Chandra laughed loudly and Ganesha's stomach burst open. It was stitched back by Pārvati who then cursed Chandra that whoever sees him shall become the subject of scandals. Brahma and the other Devas pleaded with Pārvati to rescind her curse, which she did on the condition that only on Ganesha's birthday would the curse apply. The curse would be in force on that day until the story of Ganesha was told. That was why on Ganesha's birthday this

Chandramati

Wife of Harischandra. She was put to the test by Viswāmitra who took all of the money of Harischandra and forced him to sell Chandramati and her little son Lohitasya to a Brahmin family. Chandramati became a slave mostly cleaning and washing. Lohitasya went one day to the forest and was bitten by a snake and died. Chandramati finished her chores and began searching for her son in the night. She found him dead and took him to the banks of Ganga for cremation. Harischandra had to sell himself (to pay for Viswāmitra) to the owner of the cremation sites. When Chandramati brought the body of Lohitasya, Harischandra demanded the fee for cremation, but she had no money. She was going to the city to beg and on the way some robbers dropped stolen goods into her bag. Soon the king's police found the goods in her bag and she was sentenced to be beheaded. She came to Harischandra again, and this time they recognized each other and were saddened for their lives. The king's verdict had to be fulfilled, so Harischandra raised his sword to sever Chandramati's head. Viswāmitra and other Maharishis then appeared and restored the lives of Chandramati and Lohitasya, explaining it was only a test and they all passed it. Their kingdom was also restored to them. (see Harischandra)

Chitra

Chitra was the daughter of Kubera. Budha married her and they had a son called Chaitra.

Chitrarekha

Chitrarekha was one of the Apsaras in the court of Indra. One day while she was dancing, many animals such as deer and fawns *[bambis]* came to see her dance and she was looking at them. Indra was angered because she did not pay attention to him and so cursed her to become an animal. She begged Indra to release her from the curse. Indra said she would be released when she gave birth to a child from Vibhāndaka. Chitrarekha became a deer and roamed the forest. One day when she was thirsty, she drank from a river in which the sperm of Vibhāndaka was released. She became pregnant and gave birth to a boy called Rishyasrunga who had a horn on his head. Immediately the animal became Chitrarekha again and went to Indra's court.

Chitrāngada

Chitrāngada was the daughter of Chtravāhana, King of Manipuram. She married Arjuna and bore a son with him called Babhruvāhana. (see Arjuna and Babhruvāhana)

Chitrāngada (2)

Chitrāngada (2) was the son of Santana and Satyavati. Bhīshma's half-brother, was married to Ambika but was killed in a fight with a Gandharva. (see Bhīshma, and Mahabhārata)

Dadhīchi

Dadhīchi was the son of Chyavana. While he was meditating on the banks of the Saraswati, Indra became jealous and sent an apsara called Alambusa. She seduced Dadhīchi and his sperm fell into the river. Saraswati became pregnant and bore a son who was named Sarāwata. Saraswati was ashamed of this and became an invisible river.

Dadhīchi was also a great rishi. When the Devas and the Rākshasas quarreled and the Rākshasas tried to steal all of the weapons of the Devas, the Devas came to Dadhīchi and asked him to keep their weapons secretly. Dadhīchi agreed to this, but the Devas were pleasure bound and did not come for a long time to retrieve their weapons. Meanwhile, Dadhīchi liquified all of the weapons and drank them. One day the Devas came and asked for their weapons. Dadhīchi told them they were in his body and they would have to kill him to get them. The Devas said they would not kill a Brahmin and a rishi, but they would like to have their weapons. Dadhīchi self-immolated, and from his bones came the super weapons such as Chakra and Vajra.

Daksha

Daksha was one of the Prajāpatis (those who are equal to Brahma) born of Brahma through his right thumb. He was married to Dharani (earth) who was born of Brahma through his left thumb. They had fifty daughters and five sons. The oldest daughter was Sati who married Shiva. On one occasion Brahma was performing a yagna and Daksha came to visit the yagna and there saw Shiva. Shiva did not get up to greet him, and since then Daksha and Shiva have been at odds. When Daksha was performing another yagna, he invited all of his other daughters but not Sati. Sati heard of the yagna and came on her own even after being warned by Shiva that she would not be welcome. When she appeared, Daksha scolded her and Shiva and asked her to leave. At that point she was hurt and angry, so she jumped in the fire with thoughts of Shiva. Word traveled rapidly that Sati had committed self-immolation, and Shiva was very angry. He immediately pulled one of his braids and out of that came Vīrabhadra. Shiva ordered Vīrabhadra to go and destroy Daksha, his yagna and whoever was there. Following the orders of Shiva,

Vīrabhadra went and destroyed everything and even beheaded Daksha. When his wife pleaded for mercy, Shiva attached a goat's head to Daksha's body. Daksha is also known as Ajamukha meaning goat faced. Shiva cursed Daksha to be born to a maid called Marisha and promised to cause obstacles to whatever she undertook. At this Daksha became angry and counter-cursed Shiva to lead a life of poverty until the end of time.

Daksha was born as the son of Marisha and Pracheta. When he was performing tapas, Vishnu appeared before him and presented him a wife Asakni and asked him to create the world. Daksha had several sons and daughters with Asakni and asked his sons to procreate. At that point Nārada appeared and discouraged them by asking why do they have to have families and attachments. Daksha heard this and cursed Nārada to be born to one of his daughters and also went to Brahma to complain. He cursed Nārada to not have a permanent place to live. He then gave Brahma his daughter Priya from whom Nārada was born again. Nārada was also one of the Prajāpatis and so had to be born only to Brahma.

Damayanti

Damayanti was the daughter of the king of Vidarbha. One day when she was strolling in the palace garden, a swan came and spoke in a human voice extolling the virtues of Nala. She was infatuated with him and wanted to marry him athough she could not see him. When her father declared her Swayamvara (self-selection of groom) she expected Nala to be there. Many of the Devas heard of her beauty and character and wanted to marry her. They all came as Nalas. Damayanti had difficulty in choosing the real Nala and prayed to the gods. At their inspiration, she looked at the feet of all the Nalas. There was only one touching the earth with his feet, because the Devas would not set their feet on the earth. She went to Nala and garlanded him and they were married with great pomp. Soon after this a jealous Pushkara invited Nala for a gambling match, in which Nala lost everything he had and went into the forest with Damayanti. The life in the forest was not easy or comfortable and he could not bear what he had done. Thinking that if he were to leave, Damayanti would go to her father and live in comfort. He therefore left her and walked away. Poor Damayanti searched all the forest for Nala and suddenly a snake appeared and threatened to bite her. At that very moment, a hunter came and cut the snake down. He wanted to marry Damayanti and would not listen that she was already married and was also a Pativrata (husband worshipper). When he attempted to force her, she cursed him and he was destroyed. She kept on searching and in that process she found a job as a maid-in-waiting to the queen. The queen was actually her aunt but did not recognize her. One day a Brahmin who was tasked with searching for Damayanti was visiting the queen, he recognized Damayanti and took her to her father the king of Vidarbha. All of the astrologers predicted that Nala would appear soon and take Damayanti, but there was no sign of Nala. The king decided to offer a second Swayamvara for Damayanti, hoping that Nala would somehow show up. In the mean time, Nala himself became a cook (chef) at the palace of Rutuparna, who decided to go the second Swayamvara of Damayanti. He took Nala with him; Nala was under the alias Bahuka at this time. Damayanti could guess that this Bahuka was indeed Nala and wanted to test him. She sent her children to Bahuka who recognized them right away

98

and hugged and kissed them affectionately. With this proof, Damayanti went to Nala and asked him what kind of man he was to leave his wife in the forest and walk away? Nala countered what kind of woman she was to declare herself available for a second marriage when the first one was still active? Damayanti said that it was all a ploy to get him back and at that point a heavenly voice pronounced that Dmaynati was indeed a Pativrata. Nala took his aliases off, reunited with Damayanti, and regained his empire and ruled fairly for a long time.

Danda

Danda was the youngest son of Ikshwaka and a very bad man. He would torture his playmates and sometimes kill them. Danda's father asked him to leave and go beyond the mountains. Danda did as his father asked and even built a great city on the other side and was its ruler. Danda also cultivated good relationships with Sukrā charya and became friendly with demons whose guru was Sukra. One day he saw a young beautiful woman meditating and asked her who she was and wanted to make love to her. She said she was one of Sukra's daughters and as such she was like a sister to him and should not fall in love with him. He did not listen to her and forced her to have sex with him. She told her father what had happened and he became very angry and cursed Danda that his city, along with him in it would become a heap of dirt. Out of that dirt grew a forest called Dandakāranya (Danda's forest).

Dasaradha

Dasaradha was the king of Ayodhya of the Sun dynasty and the son of Aja. He heard of the beauty of Kausalya and wanted to marry her. Kausalya's father invited Dasaradha to come and visit him and Dasaradha started the journey with all of his entourage. At the same time Rāvana also heard of the beauty of Kausalya. He kidnapped her and put her in a box and hid it. Kausalya's father (Bhānumanta) did not know what to do; he could not fight Rāvana. On the way to see Kausalya there was a great flood and the entourage of Dasaradha was scattered. Dasaradha himself was floating downstream and found a tree to hold on to. Under that tree was the box in which Kausalya was hidden. They married immediately and the great bird Jatāyuvu (a vulture) took them back to Ayodhya and Jatāyuvu became a friend of Dasaradha.

Dasaradha had two other wives Kaika and Sumitra. Once Indra asked him to join him in a fight with the demon Sambara, and Dasaradha took Kaika along with him to the battle. During the battle, the pin of Dasaradha's chariot wheel came off and Kaika boldly held the wheel with her finger. Dasaradha was pleased and asked her to choose two boons. She said she was happy and would choose when the time came.

Dasaradha had the skill of shooting in darkness; he could shoot at the sound of the object. One day when he was hunting, a little Brahmin boy was trying to take water from the river. At the sound of the water filling the vessel, Dasaradha thought it was an animal and shot the boy. When the boy screamed, Dasaradha went and found the child about to die. The boy said that his parents were blind and that they were thirsty. Dasaradha took the water to them and slowly broke the bad news. They screamed and cursed Dasaradha that he too would die screaming for his son.

Dasaradha did not have any sons, so he performed a yagna called Putrakāmeshti and the Yagnapurusha brought him a pot of Payasam (milk rice) and asked him to give it to his wives. He gave one half to Kausalya and the other to Kaika. They both in turn shared half of theirs each with Sumitra. Kausalya gave birth to Rāma, Kaika to Bharata, and Sumitra to Lakshmana and Satrughna. As the boys were growing, Viswāmitra (a great rishi) came and asked Rāma and Lakshmana to be sent with him for training and also to kill a few Rākshasas. Dasaradha hesitated first and then obliged. Viswāmitra taught Rāma and Laksmana all the sciences and arts including martial arts and showed them how to slay demons, like Tātaka and her sons Māricha and Subāha.

Later they were traveling through the kingdom of Janaka. Janaka had a daughter called Sīta and proclaimed whoever bends the bow in his basement, that person would marry her.

Rāma was asked by Viswāmitra to try, and Rāma easily lifted the bow and bent it until it broke. Janaka was pleased and sent word for Dasaradha to come for the wedding of Rāma and Sīta. The wedding was beautiful and they all returned to Ayodhya when Dasaradha decided to make Rāma the king. All the preparations were made and Dasaradha went to Kaika to ask her to attend. Kaika was influenced by Mandhara, the maid who advised her to have her son Bharata crowned king and Rāma sent to the forest. Kaika asked Dasaradha to honor his promise of granting her two

101

wishes. First she asked that Rāma be sent away to the forest for fourteen years and second Bharata (her son) be crowned as king. Dasaradha was crest fallen and speechless. Rāma heard this and said he would go to the forest and Sīta and Lakshmana also joined him. Dasaradha could not bear this and died panting for his favorite son.

Parasurāma took an oath to kill all kings for twelve months except when a king was just married. So to avoid the ax of Parasurāma, Dasaradha married a woman every day for one year.

Dāsaraj

Dāsaraj was a fisherman king and the father of Satyavati, Bhīshma's stepmother. (see Bhīshma)

Dattātreya

Dattātreya was the son of Atri and Anasuya. He was actually Vishnu who became the adopted son of Atri. He was a great rishi and had several pupils who always surrounded him. In order to seek privacy he hid in a lake. Kārtavīrya (a king) was always praising and serving Dattātreya because he knew Dattātreya was Vishnu. Once a fire generated by gas from Dattātreya burned the arms of Kārtavirya, yet Kārtavirya praised Dattātreya who restored his arms and gave him a thousand more so he could conquer all his enemies.

Devaki

Devaki was the wife of Vasudeva and the mother of Krishna. Devaki was jailed by her brother Kamsa who was afraid that her son would kill him. He insisted on killing her children as soon as they were born. In her previous life she was Aditi (wife of Kasyapa). In the first Yuga, Marichi and Varsha had six children and because of a curse they were born to Devaki and were killed immediately by her brother Kamsa. When Devaki wished to see them, Krishna and Balarāma went to the netherworld and requested of Bali that they be permitted to see their mother Devaki. As soon as she saw them, Devaki felt the motherly feeling and gave them breast milk. Immediately their curse was gone and they went to the heavens. Krishna later killed Kamsa and released his mother Devaki.

Devayāni

Devayāni was the daughter of Sukrācharya. She fell in love with Kacha, who had come to Sukra to learn about Sanjiva (reviving dead people). Kacha was the son of Bruhaspati and had been sent to learn the medicine of Sanjiva, which was known only to Sukra. He gained the confidence of the guru and learned the art and was about to take leave, when Devayāni asked him to marry her. He refused saying that a guru's daughter is like a sister and so he could not marry her. Disappointed and angry, she cursed him that his knowledge would not be applicable. He counter-cursed her that she should not be the wife of a Brahmin.

One day Devayāni and her friend Sarmishta were bathing and Sarmishta pushed Devayāni into a well after a minor quarrel. Devayāni was crying for help and a king by the name of Yayāti heard her cry and pulled her out of the well. She told her story and asked that her father be informed. When Sukra came and asked Devayāni to come home, she refused and said she would not enter the city in which Sarmishta was living. In order to be with his daughter, Sukra left the city, the ruler of which was Sarmishta's father. Devayāni also insisted that Yayāti should marry her because he pulled her by holding her right hand. When Sarmishta's father Vrushaparva heard that Sukra left the city, he begged Sukra to come back and offered Sarmishta as a slave to Devayāni. Yayāti accepted Devayāni as wife and Sarmishta as her slave, and they had two children. Yayāti also fathered two more children by Sarmishta and one of them was Pūru. When Devayāni heard of this, she was angry and immediately left Yayāti and went to her father and told him how Yayāti belittled her by sleeping with her slave. Sukra cursed Yayāti to become on old man immediately and when Yayāti begged him for mercy and convinced him that he had a lot of time to enjoy with Davayāni but could not if he were to become an old man. Sukra offered that if any one could give his youth to him, he could be youthful again. He asked all his children from Devayāni as well as Sarmishta to loan their youth to him. All refused except Pūru. Yayāti became young again and enjoyed his wives for a long time. This is why Pūru is considered to be one of the four great givers (the others were Bali, Karna, and Sibi).

Dhanya

Dhanya was the granddaughter of Daksha. When they were visiting Vishnu, they encountered the rishis Sanatkumaras. Dhanya did not pay heed to them and was thus cursed to be born as a human woman. She became the wife of Janaka and the mother of Sīta.

Dharmaja

Dharmaja was the eldest son of Kunti and Pāndu. He was actually born to Kunti and Yama. He was known as Yudhistira. After the death of Pāndu, Dharmaja became the prince and because of his fair and pleasant rule, he quickly became popular. His cousin Duryodhana hated him and was always scheming to dethrone him. Dharmaja was asked by his uncle Dhrutarāshtra to go to Varanasi. On the way, the house they were staying in was set on fire, but the five Pāndavas escaped. Next they went to Drupada's city disguised as Brahmins. When the contest for the hand of Draupadi was announced, it was to shoot down a revolving fish by looking at the reflection only. First all of the Kshatriyas were allowed to try. When no one succeeded, the Brahmins were given a chance to participate and Arjuna won the contest. When they announced to Kunti that they had won a prize, Kunti asked all five to share it. Draupadi thus became the wife of all of the Pāndavas. After spending some time in the city of Drupada, they went to Indraprastha and Dharmaja was ruling it peacefully. Duryodhana was jealous of the Pāndavas and determined to destroy them. He challenged Dharmaja to a poker game in which Dharmaja lost everything.   As a condition of losing, they had to leave Indraprastha and go to the forest for 12 years then one year without being recognized.   At the end of 13 years, Dharmaja wanted to have his land and Duryodhana refused.   The only recourse for Dharmaja and the Pāndavas was to fight for their rights.   This was the great epic battle in which the Pāndavas, especially Arjuna killed the Kauravas and regained their land.

During their life in the forests, Duryodhana wanted to humiliate Dharmaja, so he went with a large army to the forest.   On the way he was attacked by the armies of Chitrasena and taken prisoner. Dharmaja heard of this and sent Bhīma and Arjuna to defeat Chitrasena and rescue Duryodhana.   When they asked why he was ordering them to rescue their enemy, Dharmaja replied that in case of danger from outsiders, Kauravas and Pāndavas were still one family.   This was his concept of fairness.

On a hot day, Dharmaja sent Sahadeva to fetch some water from a nearby lake.   When he did not return, Nakula went and when he did not return either, Bhīma and Arjuna also went and did not return.   Dharmaja went and saw all his brothers lying unconscious on the banks of the lake.   While he was examining them, a voice called to him and said if he could answer several questions, he would be able to revive his brothers.   He answered all the questions put by Yaksha, and when asked to choose any one of his brothers, Dharmaja chose Nakula's life.   Yaksha wondered and asked him why he chose Nakula instead of Arjuna or Bhīma because they could help him gain his empire.   Dharmja's reply was that he was the son of Kunti, and one of Mādri's sons should also live.   At that noble and fair judgment, the Yaksha was pleased and revived all the brothers.

During the year of incognito, all of the Pāndavas enterd the kingdom of Virāta under different names. Dharmaja assumed the name Kankubhat and secured a job as a jester and adviser. When the year was over and Virāta found out who these people were, he treated them with great respect.

During the war, Drōna became the commander after Bhīshma and there wasn't anyone who could kill Drōna (he was the guru). Dharmaja went and uttered loudly that Aswatthāma died and silently the word elephant. Aswatthāma was the son of Drōna and there was also an elephant by the same name. When Drōna heard Aswatthāma and not the word elephant, he presumed his son died and fainted and was killed by Drushtadyumna.

Since all of his cousins and relatives died in the war, Dharmaja began to perform the rituals (for dead people), and at that moment Kunti asked him to perform first for Karna because he was his older brother. Dharmaja was shocked and saddened to know that the great Karna was his older brother. He cursed that women could never keep a secret.

After ruling for several years and performing some yagnas, Dharmaja finally made Abhimanya's son Parīkshit the king and retired to the mountains. One day as they were all (five pandavas and Draupadi) climbing to reach Kailas, a dog followed them. One by one they all fell and died because they all had some type of weakness. First was Sahadeva - he thought he was the most handsome; Nakula - he was too proud of his knowledge of horses;

Bhīma - he was too fond of eating and too proud of his strength; Draupadi - she was unfairly partial in her love for Arjuna; Arjuna - he was too proud of his abilities as an archer. When they were all gone only Dharmaja and the dog were able to go to Kailas. Indra came with his chariot and asked Dharmaja to come with him. Dharmaja asked the dog to climb into the chariot first and Indra protested, but Dharmaja said the dog was the only faithful companion he had towards the end and if the dog could not go then he too would not go. At that moment the dog became Yama and blessed Dharmaja and he went to heaven.

Dharmaja was looking for his brothers in heaven, but did not find them. Instead he found all the Kauravas. He wanted to see his brothers and was told they were all in hell. He went to hell and asked to be allowed to stay in hell as long as his brothers were there, but was told that was only an illusion. Actually he could join his brothers in heaven after he bathed in Ganga at Kailas, which he did and happily joined all his brothers including Karna.

Dharmavyādha

Dharmavyādha was a butcher selling meats in the city of Mithila. He knew all of the Vedic rituals and led a very disciplined life. Kausika, a Brahmin, learned the wisdom about life and nonviolence from Dharmavyādha. (see Kausika) Dharmavyādha was actually a great Brahmin in a previous life. He was a friend of many princes and was adept at the martial arts. One day he went to the forest accompanied by his friends and there he shot a hermit mistaking his sounds for those of an animal. The hermit thus cursed him to become a butcher.

Dharmavrata

Dharmavrata was the daughter of Dharma and the wife of Mārichi. She was also a great Pativrata (absolute dedication to husband). One day she was stroking her husband's feet while he was sleeping and Brahma came to visit them. She was puzzled for a while whether or not to disturb her husband and greet her father-in-law (Brahma). She decided to get up and welcome Brahma and at that time her husband woke up and thought she was with another man, and cursed her to become a stone. She was angry at her husband because she was only greeting Brahma and so she counter-cursed Mārichi that he would be destroyed by Shiva. In order to get out of their curses, both Dharmavrata and Mārichi began tapas. Finally Brahma appeared before her and gave her the boon that whoever touched her as a stone, they would go to the heavens and so would their ancestors if rituals for them were performed at the stone. Dharmavrata became a stone statue (Devarūpini) and Brahma installed that statue in Gaya. (see Mārichi)

Dhrutarāshtra

Dhrutarāshtra was the son of Ambika by Vyāsa. Ambika was the widow of Vichitravīrya and was childless. Her mother-in-law Satyavati asked her firstborn son Vyāsa to produce a child to rule as successor to Santana. Upon seeing Vyāsa the great bearded hermit, Ambika was afraid and closed her eyes during copulation. Their son Dhrutarāshtra was thus born blind. He was taught all

109

the martial arts and secrets of administration by Bhīshma (his uncle) and was made king. He married Gāndhāri and they had one hundred sons the eldest of which was Duryodhana. When Duryodhana succeeded to the throne, he was cruel to the Pāndavas and Dhrutarāshtra could not influence him to do otherwise. When the Great War was over, he retired to the forest with Gāndhāri, Kunti, and Vidura (his half-brother) and lived a peaceful life until a fire engulfed them and they all perished.

Dhrutarāshtra was not quite neutral in the matters between the Pāndavas and the Kauravas. For some reason he condoned all of the bad things that were inflicted on the Pāndavas. He was also a very strong man. After the war when Bhīma called on him, he asked Bhīma to come near so he could hug him. Krishna pulled Bhīma to the side and pushed a steel statue in front of Dhrutarāshtra, which he hugged and crushed. Actually he wanted to crush Bhīma to avenge his son Duryodhana who was killed by Bhīma.

Although he was blind, Krishna gave him one time vision to see him and the splendor of the universe.

Dhruva

Dhruva was the son of King Uttānapada and Suniti. His stepmother was Suruchi. One day when he was sitting on his father's lap, Surichi came and pushed him away saying only her son has the right to sit on the king's lap. Dhruva felt belittled and angry and left the palace to perform tapas. On his way Nārada taught him some mantras and he learned a great deal from the seven Maharishis. He prayed to Vishnu who gave him many boons. Upon hearing all of this news, Uttānapada welcomed Dhruva back and made him the king. Dhruva treated his stepmother and her son with proper respect, but his half-brother quarreled with many and was killed by a Yaksha. Dhruva attacked the Yakshas and Kubera and defeated them. He reigned peacefully for a very long time and became a star in the sky after his death. This star is known as Dhruva Nakshatra, the Pole Star.

Dilipa

Dilipa was a king of the Ikshwaka dynasty and an ancestor of Rāma (great, great, great grandfather). As he and his wife had no children, they consulted the rishi Vasishta and found out they had a curse by the golden cow Kāmadhenu. Vasishta asked them to serve Kāmadhenu's daughter Nandini. They were diligently taking care of Nandini and one day she went into a lion's den. Dilipa immediately attempted to draw his arrow to kill the lion, but his arm froze. The lion spoke in a human voice saying that it was hungry and Nandini was a good meal. Dilipa asked the lion to spare Nandini and instead have him for a meal. Nandini was so pleased and told Dilipa that was all an illusion to test him and he could have his wish, which was to have a son. That son was Raghu.

Diti

Diti was the daughter of Daksha and Dharani (Earth) and the wife of Kasyapa. She had three rivals Aditi, Vinata, and Kadruva. She was very sexual and always copulated at dusk. Kasyapa cursed her that her sons would become demons and would torture the earth, and Vishnu would kill them because no one else could. The great Hiranyāksha and Hiranyakasipa were her children. All demons are her children and they are called Daityas (Diti's children).

Draupadi

Draupadi was the daughter of Drupada. Arjuna won her hand in a contest and by a strange coincidence she became wife of all the five Pāndavas. When the question arose of how to be a wife to all five at the same time, Nārada resolved it that Draupadi should spend one year with each of the Pāndavas and thus rotate her being a wife to all of them. She gladly obliged and was very respectful of them all. She was lost in a gambling bet and was humiliated by Duryodhana, but kept her cool and Krishna prevented her from being disrobed by Dussāsana. She endured all of this and led a faithful life to the Pāndavas. She was one of the three great wives in the hall of fame (the other two were Tāra and Mandōdari).

Dharmaja became king of Indraprastha and Draupadi was a great royal hostess. When the architect Maya built them a beautiful palace, they invited many people including Duryodhana and his brothers. In the palace, there were many illusions such as a lake when there was none and a park when it was actually a lake. Duryodhana became confused and pulled his clothing up thinking there was water, and stepped into water when it appeared as a park. Draupadi saw this and laughed. Duryodhana was angered by her insult and vowed to destroy her and the Pāndavas. The rift started this way and soon Duryodhana invited Dharmaja for a gambling session in which he lost everything including Draupadi. Draupadi was dragged into the court and humiliated.

Draupadi followed her husbands into the forest and into the year of incognito in the service of Virāta. She was assaulted by Kīchaka, the brother-in-law of Virāta. She told Bhīma of the incident and they both conspired to gain revenge upon Kīchaka. They lured Kīchaka to a secret place after dark and there Bhīma, instead of Draupadi grabbed Kīchaka and crushed him to death.

When the time came to negotiate with the Kauravas about their kingdom, Krishna was sent as the mediator. Draupadi sought Krishna and told him how she had endured all of the humiliations and she would like to see the negotiations fail. She wanted war so that the Pāndavas could annihilate all of the Kauravas. Surely her desire was fulfilled.

113

Drōna

Drōna was the son of Bharadwāja and Ghrutāchi. He grew up at his father's ashram and learned all of the Vedas. Drupada was his friend and also the prince of Pānchala. They both learned all of the martial arts together. Drōna married Krupi and their son was Aswatthāma. They had a great deal of knowledge and many skills, but no money. They were so poor they couldn't afford milk for their little son. Drōna went to Parasurāma because he heard that Parasurāma was giving away the wealth of his vanquished kings. By the time Drōna arrived, all of the wealth had been given away. Drōna served Parasurāma and learned special archery skills from him. Drōna remembered his boyhood friend Drupada who had become king by then, and called on him. Drupada insulted him and taunted him that poor Brahmins and kings had nothing in common. Humiliated, Drōna went to Hastinapura. There he saw a group of boys trying to get a ball that had fallen in a well. Drōna told them he could get it out and showed them how. He shot an arrow into the ball first and then another arrow into that arrow and another into that one and thus built a long rod of arrows and pulled the ball out. The boys were impressed and told the story to their father Dhrutarāshtra and uncle Bhīshma because the boys were none other than the Kauravas and the Pāndavas. Immediately Bhīshma sent for Drōna and asked him to be the guru of these boys.

Drōna taught all the boys well and trained them as warriors. He was particularly fond of Arjuna and so when the education was complete, he asked Arjuna to go and bring Drupada in chains as Gurudakshina. Drōna was fond of the Pāndavas but he remained loyal to Duryodhana who was his king and patron. When the Great War broke out, Drōna was the commander-in-chief after Bhīshma. He was slaying the Pāndava armies mercilessly. There was no way to defeat him. Krishna knew that if he were to hear that his son had died, he would faint and then could be killed. Krishna suggested that Dharmaja should go to him and utter the words loudly that Aswatthāma had died, and since Dharmaja never told untruth, he should add the word elephant in a low tone of voice because there indeed was an elephant by that name and it had died. When Drōna heard the news that Aswatthāma had died but not the word elephant, he fainted and fell. Drushtadyumna immediately killed him to avenge his father's humiliation.

Drupada

Drupada was the king of Pānchala and the father of Draupadi. He was actually the son of Vrushata and Menaka. When Vrushata was meditating, Menaka came by collecting flowers. He fell in love with her and the result was Drupada who was left in the ashram of Bharadwāja. He grew up with Bharadwāja's son Drōna and became a great warrior. When his father died, he became king of Pānchala and had a son and a daughter. The daughter was Draupadi and the son was Drushtadyumna. One day when Drōna was in need of money, he approached his boyhood friend Drupada and was insulted by him. He went away and trained Arjuna and asked him to bring Drupada in chains, which Arjuna did. Drōna admonished him and let him go. He performed a great sacrifice seeking a son who would kill Drōna and a daughter who would marry Arjuna. He got a son Drushtadyumna and a daughter Draupadi. After learning that the Pāndavas including Arjuna were traveling and had become lost, he proclaimed a ritual in which a device engineered by him with a revolving fish that could be shot by looking at its reflection would be the test for his daughter's hand. Arjuna in the disguise of a Brahmin shot the fish and became her husband. When Drōna fell after hearing the news that his son had died, Drushtadyumna went ahead to Drōna's fallen body and severed his head as revenge for his father's humiliation.

Drushtadyumna

Drushtadyumna was the son of Drupada and brother of Draupadi. He fought on the side of the Pāndavas and when Drōna fell, he cut his head off to fulfill a promise to his father.

Dūrvasa

Dūrvasa was a great rishi and the son of Atri and Anasūya. He was famous for his quick anger and cursing. Dūrvasa was also a great giver of mantras. He gave Kunti the power to call on any god and have her desire fulfilled. Kunti could get her children from different gods; Karna from Sun, Dharmaja from Yama, Arjuna from Indra, and Bhīma from Vāyu.

Duryodhna

Duryodhna was the eldest son of Dhrutarāshtra and Gāndhāri. He was the villain of Mahabhārata, always conniving to destroy the

Pāndavas. Duryodhna was also a great warrior and specialist at gada (club) fighting. He was jealous of the Pāndavas and was determined to destroy them, especially after he visited their palace in Hastinapuram and was insulted by Draupadi. He schemed and called Dharmaja for a gambling match and tricked him into losing. The conditions were that the loser would go for twelve years into the wilderness and for one year remain incognito, and if discovered they would have to repeat the entire cycle. Dharmaja lost all of his wealth, and even his wife Draupadi was dragged into the court and humiliated. At the end of the year of incognito, Dharmaja asked for his empire and was refused. He asked to have five villages for himself and his brothers so there would not be a fratricidal war. Duryodhana refused even that saying he would not give them even one phead of land. All mediators failed and the Great War ensued in which all the Kauravas including Duryodhana were killed.

After seeing Arjuna and his skills as an archer, Duryodhana wanted to have someone who could match the skills of Arjuna. He found Karna and made him a prince so that he would have the same rank to fight Arjuna. When Karna fell and Salya took over and was also killed, Duryodhana hid himself in the ocean. Krishna called him and even taunted him to come out and prove himself and die like a king. He could even choose with whom to fight. Duryodhana came out and chose to fight with Bhīma. That was the great gada battle between the two in which Bhīma hit him below the belt on the thigh and felled him.

Just before the battle, Duryodhana's mother Gāndhāri asked him to come to her naked. Krishna heard this and quickly told him he was a grown man and should not go naked to his mother, and

117

advised him to wear a loincloth around his hips. When Duryodhana went to see his mother, she affectionately rubbed all his body and found he was wearing a piece of cloth and knew immediately he would be vulnerable there. She transmitted her power to his body and made it unbeatable except for the part that was covered. In the battle with Bhīma, Krishna signaled to Bhīma that he should hit Duryodhana in the groin even though it was illegal. Bhīma hit him in the groin and felled him after which he kicked his head with his feet.

After the death of Duryodhana, Krishna consoled the Pāndavas for their killing of the enemy in unjust ways, by telling them that the Kauravas were also great warriors and the only way to beat them was by illegal means. Bhīshma was disarmed by putting a eunuch before him, Drōna was felled by lying about the news of the death of his son, Karna was felled when he was lifting his chariot without any weapon, and Duryodhana was felled when he was hit below the belt on the thighs, all illegal means.

Dussāsana

Dussāsana was one of the sons of Dhrutarāshtra and the brother of Duryodhana. He was the one who dragged Draupadi and tried to strip her of her clothes. Krishna protected her honor by providing her with a neverending sari. Witnessing this Bhīma vowed to kill Dussāsana, rip open his heart, and drink his blood, which he did.

Dwādasaditya(s)

Dwādasaditya was one of the twelve different names of the Sun. Although there is only one Sun, he rules every month under a different name with a different entourage. The Indian calendar starts with its first month corresponding to April. *Perhaps this is the reason that horoscopes also start with Aries and April.*

In April the Sun assumes the name Dhāta, in May Aryama, in June Mitra, in July Varuna, in August Indra, in September Vivaswanta, in October Tvashta, in November Vishnuvu, in December Taryama, in January Bhaga, in February Pusha, and in March Kratuvu.

119

Dwāraka

Dwāraka was Krishna's city and was created by Viswakarma. During a fierce battle with two kings Kalāyana and Jarāsndha, Krishna was afraid and so asked Viswakarma to build a city that was impenetrable. When asked where to build this city, Krishna prayed to the seas, and was given a piece of land 18 miles wide and 30 miles long. Viswakarma created Dwāraka on this piece of land. Many of the Deavas gave gifts to the city; a great hall by Indra, horses by Varuna, gold by Kubera, and gardens by the kings of the heavens. Balarāma evacuated all the citizens of Mathura to Dwāraka. Arjuna was a frequent guest in Dwāraka.

Ekalavya

Ekalavya was the son of the hunter King Hiranyadhanva. Ekalavya knew of the fame of Drōna as a great teacher of archery and went to him and asked to become his pupil. Drōna refused because Ekalavya was neither a Brahmin nor a Kshatriya. Ekalavya was disappointed and took leave of Drōna respectfully. He created a statue of Drōna with clay and taught himself the archery. One day when the Pāndavas and the Kauravas were hunting in the forest, they met Ekalavya and wondered at his skill. Even Arjuna felt jealous that there was one greater than him. They went back to the city and told Drōna about Ekalavya. Drōna went to see him and Ekalavya respectfully bowed at Drōna's feet and told how he taught himself in front of the statue of Drōna. A bewildered Drōna thought for a moment and to keep Arjuna as the greatest, asked Ekalavya to give him his Gurudakshina (teacher fee). Ekalavya replied to name whatever Drōna wanted. Drōna asked Ekalavya to give him his right thumb. Without hesitation Ekalavya cut his thumb off and gave it Drōna thus loosing all his archery skill.

Gandāki

Gandāki was a river flowing south from the Himalayas. Small rocks found in this river were called Saligramas (Shiva symbols). When Shiva was making love to Jaganmohini, she was sweating and that sweat became Gandāki and the stones found in that river were the Saligramas.

Gāndhāri

Gāndhāri was the wife of Dhrutarāshtra and the mother of the Kauravas. When she found out that her husband was blind, she blindfolded herself and never saw light again. She was pregnant at the same time as Kunti, but there were no children even after a year into the pregnancy. When she heard that Kunti had a child, she bent her womb so hard that a blob of flesh came out and she was saddened. At that time Krishnadwaipāyana came to her and said that from that blob would come one hundred sons and one daughter. She divided it into 101 parts and out of those parts were born Duryodhana, Dussāsana...one hundred sons, and Dussila a daughter.

Sakuni was Gāndhāri's brother and was a cunning gambler who helped Duryodhana win the gambling match with Dharmaja.

121

Gāndhāri was saddened at what her sons did to Draupadi and tried to convince them it was wrong, but they never heeded. At the end of the war, she wished to protect Duryodhana and asked him to come to her naked so she could bless his body to become indestructible. Krishna advised Duryodhana to wear something around his hips because he was a grown man, and that was where he was hit and felled. After the war, she accompanied her husband into the forest and was killed in a forest fire along with her husband Vidura, and Kunti.

Gāndiva

Gāndiva was the great bow of Arjuna given to him by Agni. When Agni was consuming the forest of Khāndava with all of its contents, Indra was sending clouds and rain to prevent Agni's progress. Agni requested Arjuna and Krishna help him and when they expressed they did not have any weapons, Agni gave the bow Gāndiva to Arjuna and Chakra the fiery wheel to Krishna. The fighter using Gāndiva could not be defeated. As Arjuna was climbing the Himalayas just before his death Gāndiva was taken away from him by Agni.

Ganesha

Ganesha was the son of Shiva and Pārvati. One day Pārvati was taking a bath and before the bath she rubbed her body with oil and applied rice paste. She peeled off the paste and made a small male statue with it and poured life into it. A small boy appeared before her and she instructed the boy to guard the gate at the front of the house and not to let anyone in. She finished her bath and was relaxing and waiting for her husband Shiva. Meanwhile Shiva came home for lunch and wanted to go in but the boy would not let him in. Shiva cut his head off and went in. Pārvati greeted him and Shiva asked who the boy was at the gate. Oh, I almost forgot, he is our boy, I made him this morning and I should ask him to come in and greet you. Shiva told her that the boy had stopped him from coming in and after some argument he had severed the head of the boy. Pārvati was saddened, and wouldn't eat or sleep. Shiva called in his Ganas (guard troops) and ordered them to fetch the head of any creature that was sleeping with its head to the north. They searched and found an elephant lying with his head facing the north. They cut off the head of the elephant and brought it to Shiva. Shiva immediately attached it to the body of the boy and lo and behold the boy stood up with the elephant head. Shiva made him the leader of the Ganas, thus the name Ganesha.

Shiva gave him the power to remove any hurdle in a task, and that is why all Hindus pray to Ganesha before any task.

When Ganesha was guarding the house of Shiva, Parasurāma came to visit and Ganesha would not let him in. A brief battle ensued in which Ganesha lifted Parasurāma with his trunk and whirled him around, and Parasurāma took his ax and cut off one of the tusks of Ganesha. At that time Shiva and Pārvati came and established peace. Since then one of Ganesha's names is Ekadanta meaning one-tusked.

Ganga

Ganga was a river and also Shiva's second wife. She was brought to earth by Bhagīratha, thus she was also known as Bhāgirathi.

124

She married Santana and their son was Bhīshma. Once at a great meeting at the court of Indra, Ganga came as a woman and Mahabhisha gazed at her lustfully and Brahma saw it and cursed Mahabhisha to be born as a mortal on earth. Ganga followed and on the way she saw the Vasuvu's and asked them where they were going. They said they were cursed by Vasishta and were going to earth to be born as mortals. (see Vasishta) They also said they knew that Mahabhisha would be born as Santana and she would marry him. They begged to be her children and also asked to be drowned right away because they did not like the earth life. When Ganga said as mother it would be difficult for her to kill all her children soon after their birth, they said that the last of her children would live a long time. The last son was Bhīshma. When Santana fell in love with Ganga, she said she would marry him if he would do everything as she wished and the moment he did not she would leave him. He agreed and she said he should bring all their offspring to her soon after the birth and she would drown them. Sanatana did that seven times and the eighth time he refused and Ganga left him. That eighth child was Bhīshma.

Ganga was brought to earth by Bhagīratha who wanted to sanctify his ancestors who were killed by Kapila. (see Bhagīratha)

Once after a great flood Ganga expanded into Kailas (Shiva's abode) and Shiva was angry and cursed her to be born as an earth woman. When she begged him to rescind the curse, Shiva said he too would be born as a human. He married Ganga and hid her in his hair. Pārvati found this out and scolded Ganga. Ganga left and went to her parent's home and there was no water anywhere. Pārvati couldn't bathe or even shower and complained to Shiva. Shiva sent Ganesha to Ganga to beg her to come back, which she did. Pārvati also made friends with her.

Garuda

Garuda was the mighty eagle on which Vishnu rode. He was also known as Garuthmanta. Garuda was the son of Kasyapa and Vinata. He saw that his mother Vinata was a slave for Kadruva and asked her why it was so. Upon learning that she lost a bet with Kadruva and a condition of the bet was she would become a slave to her, Garuda went to Kadruva and asked her what it would take to free his mother from her slavery. Kadruva replied that if he could get the nectar from Indra and feed it to her children the snakes so that they would become immortal, she would let his mother go free. Garuda set out to conquer Indra and get the nectar. Garuda first touched the feet of his father Kasyapa, who blessed him and suggested that he should eat a big turtle called Kachhapa to get enough strength and not be hungry during the fight. The nectar was heavily guarded so Garuda prayed to Brahma to give him the secret of getting close to it. After learning that secret and gaining enough strength, he went and took the pot of nectar from Indra. Indra tried to put up a fight but soon recognized the strength of Garuda and asked him nicely what he was going to do with the nectar. Garuda said that he would leave the pot at the home of Kadruva on a seat covered by darbhas (sawgrass) and Indra could take it back or share it with the snakes. He took the nectar to Kadruva and relieved his mother Vinata of her slavery. Meanwhile the snakes were preparing to taste the nectar and went to bathe to purify themselves, and left the nectar unguarded. At the same time Indra seized the

126

opportunity and stole the nectar. The snakes returned and found that the nectar was gone but licked the sawgrass in a vain attempt to taste nectar. The sawgrass split their tongue,s and that is why snakes have split or forked tongues.

When Kasyapa was performing a sacrifice, several rishis came to visit him and participate in the ritual by bringing flowers. They were tired from gathering the flowers and Indra laughed at them. They became angry and cursed that the son to be born to Kasyapa would be stronger than him and defeat him. Indra was afraid that his position would be jeopardized, and so begged Kasyapa to save him. Kasyapa said that he could not reverse what the rishis said. He would though see that his son became Indra of the birds and he would be the ride for Vishnu, thus protecting Indra and his position. Garuda is also known as Pakshīndra, meaning lord of the birds.

Once Garuda caught a snake called Maninaga, which was a deciple of Shiva. Shiva asked Nandi to go and tell Vishnu to order Garuda to release Maninaga. When Garuda refused, Vishnu cursed him that his strength would be gone. Garuda begged him to reverse the curse and Vishnu told him to pray to Shiva. Shiva instructed Garuda to bathe in Gautami (river Godāvari) and he would gain his strength back, which he did. This place is known as Garudathīrtha and believers bathe there to gain their strength back.

Garuda was catching, injuring, and eating snakes at will, a revenge for his mother's slavery. The snakes gathered and negotiated a deal that Garuda would be sent a snake a day for him to eat and in return would not harm others. One day Jīmuthavāhana wanted to rescue a snake and so offered himself as food for Garuda. Garuda did not recognize that Jīmuthavāhana was a man and after discovering this he restored him to life by giving him nectar and also at his request restored life to all the snakes he had killed. (see Jīmuthavāhana)

Gautama

Gautama was a great rishi and the husband of Ahalya. Indra and Surya (Sun) went to Gautama's ashram when he was not there and seduced Ahalya. Two sons were born to Ahalya and Gautama thought they were his sons, but Ahalya told him that they were not his. Angrily he cursed them to become monkeys and they were Vāli and Sugrīva.

Later Indra came again as a rooster in the night and crowed. Gautama thought it was time to go to the river for his morning rituals, but discovered it was still night. When he returned he saw Ahalya and Indra in bed and cursed them. Ahalya would become a stone and Indra would have his body covered with vaginas. They begged for mercy and Gautama said Ahalya would become a woman again when Rāma's feet touched her stone, and Indra's vaginas would appear like eyes to others. (see Ahalya)

Gautama had the power of creating great harvests and during a famine many fellow rishis came to him for food and hospitality. They were also jealous of his powers and so created a pseudo cow and let her graze all his fields. When Gautama saw the cow, he brushed the cow with a sign to lead her away from the fields and the cow died. All the rishis condemned Gautama as a cow killer and refused his hospitality. When Gautama prayed to Shiva, Shiva gave Gautama one of his hairs and asked him to squeeze it on the dead cow. Suddenly the cow came to life and also became a river and that river is called Godāvari. As it came from Shiva's head, she is also known as the sister of Ganga, and because Gautama was the cause of this river it also called Gautami. (see Godāvari)

Ghantakarna

Ghantakarna was a king of demons and servant of Kubera. Ghantakarna lived in the Badari forest and would eat whoever was passing by at his mealtime. One day Krishna was passing by on his way to Kailas to see Shiva. Ghantakarna asked him where he was going and was he not afraid of the demons? Krishna replied that he was going to Kailas and so he was not afraid. Ghantakarna realized who Krishna was and prayed to him so that his curse would be lifted and he became a Brahmin again.

Ghatotkacha

Ghatotkacha was the son of Bhīma and Hidimbi. He was a great warrior and fought on the side of the Pāndavas. Ghatotkacha could assume different shapes during a battle and thus was able to destroy many of his enemies. When his force was dominant and many of the Kauravas were being killed by his illusive warfare, Karna used an extraordinary weapon given to him by Indra to kill Ghatotkacha. Even in his death, Ghatotkacha took a huge demon shape and fell on the Kauravas killing a few more. At his death Bhīma cried and was consoled by Krishna, who said that by using this great weapon on Ghatotkacha, Karna could not use it against Arjuna and so could be defeated later by Arjuna.

Ghrutāchi

Ghrutāchi was one of the Apsaras. One day she was going to call on someone at the bidding of Indra, when Viswakarma saw her and expressed his desire to enjoy her. She refused and an angry Viswakarma cursed her to be born as a sudra woman on earth at which time she counter-cursed him to be born as a worker on earth. Ghrutāchi was born as an uneducated shepherd girl. One day she was meditating and praying on the banks of Ganga in Prayaga when Viswakarma who was also born as a worker saw this beautiful maiden and suddenly remembered who she was. He made some advances to her and this time she complied and their children were farmers, carpenters, blacksmiths, and construction craftsmen.

Ghrutāchi also tried to seduce Vyāsa, but was repulsed and she ran away in the form of a dog.

Gindama

Gindama was a muni. One day he and his wife were making love in the form of two deer when Pāndu came to hunt and shot Gindama. Gindama asked Pāndu why he shot him when it was forbidden to hunt and shoot mating animals. Pāndu became angry instead of repenting and threatened to kill Gindama. At that point Gindama cursed Pāndu that he would die when he mated with his wife. This was the reason Pāndu could not mate with Kunti or Mādri and the reason he died when mating with Mādri in a weak moment.

Girija

Girija was another name for Pārvati. Girija means "born to a mountain" (giri).

Godāvari

Godāvari was a river. In the ashram of Gautama, some of his guests felt jealous of his powers to create good harvests. They created a pseudo cow and let her graze in the crop fields. When Gautama saw the cow grazing away his crops, he gestured the cow to leave, but she suddenly died. All his guests scolded him for killing a cow and refused his hospitality. Gautama prayed to Shiva and asked him to revive the cow. Shiva gave him a strand of his hair and asked him to squeeze it on the cow. Suddenly the cow came to life and took the form of a river and thus the name Godāvari (a revived cow). As Godāvari also came from Shiva's hair where Ganga sits, she is considered a sister of Ganga and also a holy river like Ganga. (see Gautama)

Guha

Guha was a fisherman king and an ardent follower of Rāma. When Rāma was going to the forest to satisfy his stepmother Kaikeyi's wish, Guha helped Rāma, Lakshmana, and Sīta cross the river Ganga. Guha saw Bharata with his army two days later and thought Bharata was going to attack Rāma, so he denied the crossing for Bharata. When Bharata explained that he was going to show his respect for Rāma and ask him to come back to become the king, Guha ferried them across the river.

Hālāhala

Hālāhala was a deadly poison that came out during churning of the ocean by the Devas and Danavas. Everyone was afraid and ran to Shiva for help. Shiva drank the poison and held it in his throat lest the universe in his stomach be destroyed. The poison was so powerful that even Shiva swooned and his neck became blue. This was why Shiva was also known as Nīlakantha (Blue Necked). This happened on the new moon day in February, and most Hindus stay awake all night on that night or at least until midnight when Shiva had recovered. (see Shiva)

Hamsa

Hamsa was the son of Brahmadatta and the brother of Dibhaka. The brothers were very close and they were also friends of Jarāsandha. They prayed to Shiva and obtained many boons, one of which was that they could not be defeated. Once they went hunting in the forest and came upon the rishi Dūrvāsa. They ridiculed him for his way of life and he became angry and asked

Krishna to kill them. Krishna knew that they could not be defeated, so he devised a plan to whisper in Dibhaka's ear that Hamsa died. Dibhaka became distraught and drowned himself. Upon hearing the news of Dibhaka's death, Hamsa too became sad and killed himself by jumping off a cliff.

Hanumān (Anjaneya)

Hanumān (Anjaneya) was the son of Anjana and Vāyu and also known as Hanumantha. Anjana was the wife of Kesari, a noble monkey who after several years of marriage decided to go into solitude. Kesari asked Anjana to pray to Vāyu. Anjana did this and one day Vāyu appeared before Anjana and gave her Shiva's sperm, which he had kept with him. From this Anjana gave birth to Anjaneya. Anjaneya mistook the Sun for a fruit and wanted to eat it, but Rahu intervened. Anjaneya wanted to eat Rahu who fled to Indra and told of the boy's strength. Indra came to punish the boy on his elephant, Airavata. Anjaneya jumped on the elephant and Indra struck him with Vajra and that hit him on the hanus (cheek bones) and Anjaneya fainted. The name Hanumān comes from this incident. Vāyu saw this and was angry with Indra and removed himself from the world. The world had no air and complained to Brahma. Brahma saw what had happened and praised Vāyu. Vāyu returned with his son Anjaneya and all the Devas gave him lots of boons.

Hanumān wanted to learn from the Sun and asked the Sun to teach him. When Sun said he was always moving, he stood still occupying the east and the west. Sun admired his strength and taught him. Hanumān was a scholar in music also. He became chief of staff to Sugrīva who was banished by Vāli. When Rāma was searching for his wife Sīta, Hanuman met him and took him to Sugrīva. Sugrīva said if Rāma could kill his brother Vāli and restore his kingdom of Kishkindha to him, he would help him find Sīta. From that meeting on, Hanumān was a faithful servant to Rāma. Rāma killed Vāli and Sugrīva sent troops in all directions to search for Sīta. Rāma knew from the beginning that Hanumān would be the one to find Sīta, so he gave his wedding band to Hanumān as proof for Sīta. They searched and searched but could not find even a trace of her when Sampāti (a vulture) told them that Ravana kidnapped her and took her to Lanka.

Hanumān jumped the ocean to land in Lanka and there he found Sīta sitting under a tree surrounded by Rāvana's servant women. He saw Sīta and showed her the ring Rāma had given him. Rāvana found out that a monkey had entered his empire and ordered the monkey to be brought before him. When Hanumān did not show respect to Rāvana, he ordered that a rag be tied to Hanumān's tail and set on fire. After that was done, Hanumān jumped from one building to another setting each on fire with his burning tail. Finally after setting half of Lanka on fire, Hanumān jumped back and reported to Rāma that he had seen Sīta and how she was.

Soon there was a war between Rāma and Rāvana and Hanumān played a great role as the commander of all the monkey troops. Because Rāma had no chariot or vehicle, Hanumān carried Rāma into the battlefield on his shoulders.

On one occasion, when Lakshmana was injured and had fainted, it was Hanumān who brought the medicine mountain to revive Lakshmana. A bridge had to be built across the ocean to lead the monkey army into Lanka. All of the great monkeys were bringing rocks and dumping them in the ocean to form a bridge. There was another monkey called Nīla, who was receiving whatever Hanumān brought with one hand only. Hanumān was angry that all he could bring was handled with one hand by Nīla. Next time he brought so many rocks as he had hair by tying one rock to each hair. Even then Nīla was stretching only one hand and Rāma saw this and signaled Nīla to use both hands to keep peace and not antagonize Hanumān. After the war was over, Hanumān went with Rāma to Ayodhya and stayed there for a long time.

Once when Bhima was searching for lotus flowers for Draupadi, Hanumān stood in the way stretching his tail across the path. When asked by Bhīma to fold it and get out of his way, Hanumān replied to Bhīma to come and lift it for himself. Bhīma tried first with a few fingers, then with one hand and then with both and still could not move Hanumān's tail. He soon recognized it was Hanumān, also a son Vāyu and thus his half-brother and paid his respects.

Hari

Hari was one of the names of Vishnu.

Hari (2)

Hari was a vicious demon who prayed to Vishnu and obtained boons from him. One of these boons was that there would be a well in his town in which any corpse when dipped would give rise to ten such persons. Hari planned on raising a huge army of demons to conquer the Devas. He insulted Shiva and Shiva burnt him and his city including the well with his third eye.

Harischandra

Harischandra was the king of Ayodhya and the son of Thrisanku. His wife was Chandramati. For a long time they had no children, so he prayed to Varuna and they had a son, Rohita. After Rohita's birth Harischandra performed a great sacrifice in which participants included Viswāmitra, Adhvarya, Bhrugu, Brahma, Jamadagni, and Vasishta was the principal priest. Harischandra was known to have always told the truth. One day there was a

137

discussion about his never lying and Viswāmitra vowed to test him. He came to him one day and asked for money to perform a big sacrifice. Harischandra gave him all he wanted and Viswāmitra said he would take it when he needed it.

Time went by and Harischandra went hunting because some animals were growing in number and destroying the crops. As he was resting after a long hunt, two women came by and danced to please him. When he offered a gift, they refused and asked him to make love to them. Harischandra told them that he was a married man and faithful to his wife and he could not fulfill their wish. Angered, they went to Viswāmitra and complained, so Viswāmitra came to Harischandra and accused him of insulting his adopted daughters and he should do as they wished if he would like to apologize. Harischandra said that he would rather give all his wealth and kingdom than to betray his wife. Viswāmitra asked for that and when Harsichandra gave him all he had, he reminded Harischandra of the money for the sacrifice. Harischndra said he did not have any money left and he would get it in a few days. Viswāmitra agreed and sent his pupil Nakshatraka to collect the money as Harichandra was going to Kasi (Varanasi). On the way Nakshatraka tortured them and taunted him to say he never promised Viswāmitra anything, and the whole affair would be over.

Harischandra went to Kasi and there he sold his wife Chandramati as a servant to a Brahmin family. There was still not enough money so he sold himself as a servant to Virabāhu, a lower caste man who was also the keeper of funeral sites. With this money he paid the debt to Viswāmitra. Viswāmitra was still not happy, he was still determined to make Harischandra tell a lie. He had Rohita killed by snakebite, and poor Chandramati worked all day and after finishing her duties in the night took her son's dead body to the funeral site, but she had no money to pay for the funeral fee. Harischandra pointed out that she had a wedding necklace that she could sell and bring him the funeral fee. Chandramati was surprised because only her husband could see her wedding necklace. They both recognized each other and cried for Rohita. Harischandra said there was no way other than selling the necklace to get the funeral fee.

Chandramati started to go into town and on the way some robbers stole jewels from the palace and to escape the police, dropped those jewels into Chandramati's lap. The police arrested her and the next morning she was convicted and sentenced to be be-headed. When Chandramati was brought to the site, it was the duty of Harischandra to cut off her head even though he knew she was innocent. He proceeded to do his duty and raised the sword. At that moment all the rishis and Viswāmitra appeared and said it was all a scheme only to test him and they even resuscitated Rohita back to life. Harischandra got his kingdom back and ruled peacefully and fairly for a long time.

In Kasi (Varanasi) on the banks of Ganga, there was an area called Harischandraghat where bodies are cremated even to this day. The word Satya Harischandra comes from this for those who never tell lies (satya means truth).

Hayagrīva

Hayagrīva was another name for Vishnu. After a long fight with the demons, a tired Vishnu was resting with his head on a bow that was stretched. Everybody was looking for Vishnu and finally found him sound asleep. The Devas, Brahma, and Shiva were all there but no one wanted to wake Vishnu. Shiva came with a plan that if the bow could be unstretched, then Vishnu would wake as the bow snapped straight. They asked Vamri, a small insect to nibble at the bowstring. When this happened the bow snapped violently and severed the head of Vishnu. (see Lakshmi for a curse) Everyone was saddened and prayed to Devi who advised them to take a head of a horse and attach it to the body. They asked Viswakarma to create a horse head then attached it to Vishnu's body. This was the reason for Vishnu to be known as Hayagrīva. He also had to kill a demon by the same name.

Hayagrīva (2)

Hayagrīva (2) was a demon who prayed to Devi and asked that he would become immortal. Devi said that was not possible and he should ask for a different boon. He asked that he would be killed by someone with the same name, which she granted. Hayagrīva immediately went to torture the Devas and wreak havoc with them. Vishnu also became Hayagrīva and slew the demon.

Hema

Hema was the wife of Maya given to him by the Devas for his

great works. They had two sons Mayavi and Dundubhi and a daughter Mandōdari. Maya built a city in her honor with the same name. After some time the Devas called her back and she left Maya.

Hidimbi

Hidimbi was the sister of Hidimba a demon. The Pāndavas were camping and stopped to rest on their journey to Varanasi. Her brother asked Hidimbi to kill the Pāndavas and cook them as a meal for him. Hidimbi went to Bhīma and fell in love with him. At first Bhīma refused her, but then she promised she would serve them well and even agreed for Bhīma to kill her brother. Kunti and Dharmaja urged Bhīma to take Hidimbi as a wife. Their son was Ghatotkacha.

Himavantha

Himavantha was the king of the mountains. He performed tapas to extend his family and the Devas were pleased and asked Menaka to marry him. Their daughter was Pārvati. When Himavantha showed Pārvati's horoscope to Nārada and asked him who would be her husband, Nārada said her husband would be very poor. He would have no clothes and live in places where last rites were performed. He told them that her husband would be none other than Shiva. Himavantha and Menaka were pleased and asked Shiva to visit them. When Shiva came, Pārvati was in charge of taking care of him. Romance grew and Shiva married Pārvati and they lived in Kailas atop the Himalayan mountains.

Hiranyakasipa

Hiranyakasipa was the son of Diti and Kasyapa. He and his brother Hiranyāksha were among the most feared of the demons. In their previous lives the two brothers were gatekeepers of Vishnu and because of a curse they were born as demons and always fighting Vishnu, and eventually killed by him. They were fearless and cruel to the Devas. They were powerful and conquered all the three worlds and when Hiranyāksha tried to roll the earth and crush it, Vishnu came as a boar and killed him. Hiranyakasipa vowed to kill Vishnu, so he prayed to Brahma for a long time and obtained the boon not to die by man or animal, nor in daytime or night, not on land or in water or in the sky, not by sword or an arrow, not by any other weapon. Brahma granted him all this and then Hiranyakasipa set out to torture the worlds. He was married to Līlavati and they had a son Prahlāda who was one of the greatest devotees of Vishnu. Hiranyakasipa did not approve of this and warned his son not to mention the name Vishnu. He forbade any worship of Vishnu and when Prahlāda did not obey his orders, he tortured him. One day at dusk, Hiranyakasipa became angry and threatened Prahlāda to kill him unless he showed him where Vishnu was. Prahlāda answered that Vishnu would be anywhere he would care to look. At that point an angry Hiranyakasipa asked if Vishnu would be in a pillar, one of the many in his great palace hall. When Prahlāda said yes, he drew his sword and hit the pillar, and out came Vishnu as half-lion and half-man. Vishnu took Hiranyakasipa on his lap and ripped him to death with his claws. Hiranyakasipa means golden-bodied. The place where this happened was Simhachalam.

Hiranyāksha

Hiranyāksha was the son of Diti and the brother of Hirnyakasipa. The brothers grew up to be very powerful and conquered all of the worlds. One day Hiranyāksha began to roll the earth and tried to crush it. Everyone was frightened and prayed to Vishnu. Vishnu came as a boar and fought with Hiranyāksha and killed him by piercing his eyes with boar fangs. Hiranyāksha means golden-eyed.

Ikshawaka

Ikshawaka was the son of Vaivaswata Manu and the founder of the Ikshwaku dynasty in Ayodhya. One of his descendents was Rāma.

Ila

Ila was another name for Earth.

Ila (2)

Ila (2) was the daughter of Vāyu and the wife of Dhruva. They had a son called Utkala.

Ila (3)

Ila (3) was the daughter of Vaivaswata Manu. When Vaivaswata performed a sacrifice in order to have a son, his wife prayed for a daughter. At the end of the sacrifice, the wife stretched her hand out first and so her wish was granted and the child was a daughter, Ila. Ila was quite absent-minded. One day when she was walking in the forest, Budha saw her and fell in love with her. He took her to his ashram and she bore him a child Purūrava. (see Budha)

Ilvala

Ilvala was the son of Dūrvāsa and Ajamukhi and had a brother called Vātāpi. He prayed to the Brahmins to teach him a mantra and with that he would gain the power to rule the world. His wish was denied and so he began his revenge on the Brahmins by inviting them for a feast. Ilvala would ask his brother Vātāpi to become a goat that would be cooked and served. He would call his brother by name and Vātāpi would come out of the bellies of the Brahmins, killing them. The Brahmins approached Agastya and asked for help. Agastya agreed and went to Ilvala and enjoyed his hospitality. However, soon after the meal, before Ilvala could call his brother by name, Agastya rubbed his belly saying "digest Vātāpi digest", and Vātāpi was gone. Ilvala realized what had happened, but politely prayed to Agastya and paid his respects to the great sage. (see Agastya)

Indra

Indra was the chief of the heavens and also the lord of the East. He was born to Aditi and Vishnu was born later as his brother. His wife was Sachi. Indra rides on the white elephant Airavata and his weapon is Vazrayudha. His horse is Uchaisrava. All of these were acquired by Indra during the churning of the ocean. Actually Indra is only a title, and anyone who performed one hundred kratuvus (special sacrifices) could claim to be an Indra. Although Indra was the chief of the Devas and the heavens, he was not known for his good deeds. Indra was mostly selfish, not courageous, deceptive by using bribes or women, and frequently ran to Vishnu whenever he was attacked. After a great battle between the Devas and Danavas, the Devas were wondering how they won without realizing that Brahma was responsible. They wished to see what was the reason for their victory and so sent Agni first, and then Vāyu, but they couldn't see anything. Then Indra went and also didn't see anything first, but slowly he began to see a shape which disappeared suddenly. When Indra cried out loud who or what that was, a voice told him that it was Brahma and also the reason for their victory. Because they came close to Brahma, Indra, Agni, and Vāyu became important Devas.

Indra was the guardian of the Amruta (nectar) and Garuda took it to free his mother from her slavery because that was what Kadruva wanted. Indra used his Vazrayudha on Garuda but it did not kill him. Indra made friends with Garuda and convinced him that he should not give the nectar to Kadruva because she would give it to her children the snakes and they would live forever. Garuda said he would give it to Kadruva but Indra could steal it back from her, which he did when she sent her children to bathe in the river before they ate the nectar.

Indra wanted to marry Ahalya when she was created, but Brahma gave her to Gautama. Indra went one day as a rooster and crowed at midnight. Gautama thought it was time to go to the river for the morning ritual. In the meantime Indra came to Ahalya and was making love to her. Gautama saw it was still too dark to be early morning and so returned home to find both Ahalya and Indra together. He cursed Ahalya to become a stone and Indra to

146

wear vaginas all over his body. When Indra begged for mercy, he said they would appear as eyes to others.

Indra was killing Diti's children. Diti asked her husband Kasyapa to give her a son who would conquer Indra. Kasyapa granted her wish and Diti became pregnant. Indra found this out and tried to destroy Diti. He went to her and asked her to accept him as a servant. One day when Diti was asleep, Indra entered her womb and cut the fetus into seven pieces. When those pieces were crying, he cut each of them into seven more pieces. When all of them were crying Diti awoke and found what Indra had done. She was about to curse him and Indra begged her for mercy. She gave Indra those cut up pieces of her fetus, which became Maruttas and Indra made friends with them.

When Kunti used the mantra given to her by Dūrvāsa to have children, she prayed to Indra and had a son by him. That son was Arjuna. Indra was always trying to help his son and he knew that Karna could not be killed as long as he had his natural armor. He went to Karna disguised as a Brahmin and asked for his armor. As Karna never said no, he took his armor and gave it to Indra, but asked why would a Brahmin need his armor. Indra told him the truth and gave him a special weapon that could be used only once. It was this weapon that killed Ghatotkacha.

Indra was afraid of Kumāraswami, the biological son of Shiva and Pārvati. He tried to kill Kumāraswami by his Vazrayudha. Instead of killing Kumāra it shattered and from the dust came thousands of soldiers (Kumāraganas) and Indra fled in fear. Kuamāraswami called him back and told him he had no interest in his position or

147

his palace. Indra became friends with him and made Kumāra one his commanders.

When Sagara's sons became powerful and began to torture Brahmins and rishis, the gods were not getting their share of sacrifices. They complained to Brahma who said they would soon be destroyed. Sure enough, the sons of Sagara went with the sacrificial horse and as it entered the ocean, the water drained out. At that time Indra stole the horse and tied it in front of Kapila's ashram. Sagara's sons searched and finally found the horse in front of Kapila's ashram. They accused Kapila of stealing their horse. Kapila was disturbed from his meditation and looked at them with angry eyes that burnt them to ashes. Their ashes were redeemed much later, which sent them to the heavens. Sagra's grandson Bhagīratha prayed to Ganga and as she flowed over them they were sent to heaven. (see Bhagīratha)

Indra fought with Bali and lost. He then went to Vishnu and prayed to him to get his position back. As Bali was a righteous ruler there was no way to fight with him. Vishnu came as Vāmana (Dwarf Brahmin) and asked for three feet of land. Bali promised him the land even over the objections of Sukrācharya, his guru. Vāmana occupied the earth with one foot, the heavens with another, and asked for space for the third one. When Bali pointed out towards his head, Vāmana put his foot on his head and crushed him to the netherworld and restored Indra back to his position. (see Bali)

Indra was jealous of anyone who was performing tapas for a long time, because he was afraid they would become Indras. He used

148

all sorts of tricks to damage them. He sent Menaka to Viswāmitra to disturb his tapas, Janapadi to Saradwanta to destroy his tapas, and Pramochana to disturb Kandhu.

Once Indra got into a fight with Vrutrasura and Indra ran to Vishnu and asked for refuge. Vishnu told Indra that Vrutrasura was stronger and more powerful than him and he should make friends with him rather than fight him. One day when they were strolling on a beach, Indra sneaked up on Vrutrasura and killed him. When Vrutrasura's ghost came to haunt, Indra sought refuge in the ocean. The Devas approached Nahusha and made him Indra, but he fell from grace very quickly and was cursed to become a snake. Indra got his position back after performing purifying rituals.

Indra fought Rāvana and captured him. Rāvana's son Meghanādha received the news and so set out to fight Indra. Through his illusions and fighting skills he conquered Indra and freed his father Rāvana. Since then Rāvana's son was called Indrajit (meaning conqueror of Indra).

Indra was riding his elephant Airavata along with many Devas, and Dūrvāsa saw them and brought a flower garland for Indra. Indra put it on Airavata and the elephant dropped the garland and trampled it. Dūrvāsa felt insulted that his gift was mistreated and angrily cursed Indra that all his wealth would be drowned in the ocean. Indra again ran to Vishnu and asked for help. Vishnu said he should churn the oceans and his wealth would be returned to him. Indra arranged with both the Devas and the Danavas to churn the ocean and got his wealth back along with the poison

149

Hālāhala.

Indradyumna

Indradyumna was the King of Avanti. Seeking the truth about god, he left his kingdom and traveled south, praying to Vishnu. Vishnu appeared in his dream and told him how to obtain the statues of Trimurtis (Brahma, Vishnu, and Shiva). He traveled on and found two Brahmins resting under a banyan tree. He requested one of them to make and give him the statues of Trimurtis. One of the Brahmins was Viswakarma and he made the statues and gave them to Indradyumn who installed them in a temple and after death went to heaven.

Indradyumna (2)

Indradyumna was a princely associate of the heavens and his reputation was tarnished under false accusations and he was condemned to go to earth. He came and found everything different, so he went to the rishi Mārkandeya and asked him whether he knew who he was. Mārkandeya said he did not know but asked him to go to Pravarakarna (Great Owl). They both went to the great owl and asked the same question. The owl replied he too did not know but recommended Nalikajangha (Tall Heron). All three went to the tall heron and the heron also did not know, but suggested Kupara (Old Tortoise). When they approached the tortoise, the tortoise said yes it knew who Indradyumna was. It said that Indradyumna was a great king and performed many sacrifices and in fact the lake in which the tortoise lived was formed by the cows he gave away as they circled and trampled. At that moment the heaven's members realized they condemned an innocent one and asked Indradyumna to return to heaven.

The lake so formed is also called Indradyumnam.

Indradyumna (3)

Indradyumna was the King of Dravidas in the south. When Agastya visited Indradyumna, he did not get up from his throne. Agastya was insulted and so cursed Indradyumna to become an elephant. When he begged for mercy, Agastya said that a crocodile would catch him and Vishnu would rescue him. This was the Gajendra (king of elephants).

Indrajit

Indrajit was the eldest son of Rāvana. His original name was Meghanādha. He was an expert in maya warfare (illusionary battles) and when his father Rāvana was defeated by Indra and tied down, Meghanādha went to war with Indra, defeated him, and released Rāvana. After this he was known as Indrajit, one who conquered Indra.

When Rāma came to fight Rāvana for the release of Sīta, Rāvana's brother Vibhīshana urged Rāvana to give Sīta back to Rāma and make friends with him. Indrajit objected to this suggestion by calling Vibhīshana a coward and saying that a warrior should fight

151

and not appease. When the actual war broke out, Indrajit performed a great sacrifice on the instructions of his guru and received a golden chariot to go to battle. He rode in the chariot and killed many monkey warriors. Indrajit fought with Angada and was first defeated, but then used his trickery and captured him. Indrajit then used Nāgāstra (snake weapon) on Rāma and Laksmana and made them faint. Hanumān brought the needed medicine and revived them. He even created a false Sītā and called out to Rāma that he was going to kill her. Rāma was saddened and cried but then Vibhīshana told him the truth. Indrajit was about to complete a great sacrifice to obtain special powers that would make him unconquerable and Vibhīshana knew that. He went to Lakshmana and told him to attack Indrajit before he completed the sacrifice or else be killed by him. Lakshmana went to fight Indrajit immediately and after fierce fighting finally slew Indrajit.

Indraprastha

When the Pāndavas received their share of the kingdom, they built a city with the help of Maya and Viswakarma. That city was called Indraprastha and is known as Delhi today.

Indrasena

Indrasena was the wife of Mādgalya muni. Although Mādgalya was a leper and smelled badly, Indrasena was totally devoted to him and served him obediently. One day during a meal, one of Mādgalya's fingers fell into the bowl and Indrasena took it out and ate the rest of the food without showing any hesitation. Mādgalya was so pleased that he asked her what she would like. She said she would like sex and sexual acts if she could have them with him. By virtue of his powers, Mādgalya assumed a handsome man's shape and enjoyed sex with Indrasena on five continents and finally went back to his ashram. Indrasena still had many desires and after that life she was born as the daughter of the king of Kashi and remained a spinster for a very long time. She performed tapas vigorously praying to Shiva. Meanwhile Yama, Indra, Vāyu, and the Aswinis wanted to marry her, but she kept on praying for Shiva. Finally when Shiva appeared and asked her what she wanted, she blurted out husband five times. Shiva granted her wish and said she would have five husbands. She was born as Draupadi in the next life and her husbands were Dharmaja (son of Yama), Arjuna (son of Indra), Bhīma (son of Vāyu), and Nakula and Sahadeva (sons of the Aswinis).

Jāhna

Jāhna was the son of Munihotra and also a rishi. When he was performing a yagna (a sacrifice) Ganga followed Bhagīratha and drowned his yagna fire. Jāhna became angry and drank the Ganga, but when Bhagīratha prayed to him and explained why he was bringing Ganga (to sanctify his ancestors), Jāhna let Ganga go from his ear. This is why Ganga is called Jāhnavi.

Jalandhara

Jalandhara was a great king of Rākshasas, born out of Shiva's fury.

153

When Shiva destroyed Manmadha with his third eye, the fire from it entered the ocean and created a great explosion that terrorized the world. Brahma came to the ocean and asked what the matter was. The ocean king brought out the infant and asked Brahma to christen him and also wanted to know what future the boy would have. Brahma named the boy Jalandhara and said he would be a great king and only Shiva could kill him. As the boy grew to be a man, the ocean king sent for Kālanemi's daughter Brunda and they were married and Jalandhara became king. One day Sukrācharya, the guru of Rākshasas came to visit Jalandhara and told him how the ocean was churned and all of the goodies from it were taken away by the Devas and nothing was given to his people the Danavas. Jalandhara sent word to Indra asking him to share his wealth. Indra turned him down telling him that his brother Vishnu killed several demons like him and if Jalandhara wanted he should fight the Devas. A great battle ensued in which Vishnu was drafted to fight Jalandhara. They fought and fought and Jalandhara was not defeated. Vishnu admired Jalandhara's ability and granted him a wish. Jalandhara asked Vishnu to come with Lakshmi and stay at his palace. Vishnu did this and there was a long period of happiness. One day Nārada came to visit Jalandhara and described how beautiful Pārvati was. Immediately Jalandhara asked Pārvati to become his wife, but Pārvati refused by saying that she was like a mother to him and such thoughts would destroy him. He laughed and kept appearing wherever Pārvati went. Every time his wife Brunda also appeared and pleaded for forgiveness, and finally Pārvati sought Vishnu and asked him to seduce Brunda so that she could not protect him anymore. Jalandhara challenged Shiva to fight him and during a lull in the fight he disguised himself as Shiva and went to see Pārvati. Pārvati could see the imposter right away

154

and showed him to Shiva who then killed Jalandhara with his trident. At the same time Brunda also found out that Vishnu was trying to seduce her and cursed Vishnu to become a lifeless stone statue and was about to curse Shiva too, but Shiva appeared to her and explained the truth that Jalandhara was part of him and became part of him again and was not killed.

Jamadagni

Jamadagni was the son of Ruchika and nephew of Viswāmitra. His wife was Renuka and they had five sons the youngest of which was Parasurāma. One day Renuka was fetching water from the lake and there she saw a handsome Chitraradha swimming. She was late in bringing the water back and an angered Jamadagni asked one by one of his sons to kill their mother. Four of them refused and were cursed, but Parasurāma obediently went to his mother, took his ax, and cut her head off. Jamadagni was pleased and asked Rāma to wish for anything he wanted. Parasurāma asked for his mother to be brought back to life and his brothers freed from their curses.

Once a Hayahaya king called Kārtavirya was hunting until dark and then sought a place to rest for the night at Jamadagni's ashram. When he saw the simple ashram he said it would be too much for Jamadagni to feed and show hospitality to all of his entourage. Jamadagni said it was no problem because he had access to the sacred cow Kāmadhenu and arranged a fabulous feast for the king. A surprised Hayahaya king enjoyed the feast and asked Jamadagni to give him the cow. When Jamadagni refused, he took the cow by force and in the process killed

Jamadagni. Parasurāma was not home and his brothers couldn't do anything. When Rāma came home his mother Renuka was lying on Jamadagni's body weeping. She told Rāma what had happened and hit her forehead on the corpse twenty-one times. An angered Parasurāma vowed to kill all the kings in twenty-one raids. They were about to cremate Jamadagni's body when suddenly Bhrugu appeared and revived Jamadagni. True to his word Parasurāma went after all the kshatriyas (kings' caste) in twenty-one raids and killed most of them except those who were just married and those whose wives were about to give birth.

Jāmbavanta

Jāmbavanta was the Great Bear king born from the yawn of Brahma. He was well versed in all the sciences and rituals. He knew when Garuda was born, when the ocean was churned, and when Bali was crushed. Jāmbavanta asked the Devas for a drop of nectar and drank it. This was the reason he lived so long and was so strong. He would go around the world and stop in Kailas to chat with the munis there. When Bali's son threw a mountain at him, he stopped it with his leg. The mountain was split in two, but Jāmbavanta's leg was injured and he lost some of his strength. He helped Rāma in his fight to get Sītā back. Jāmbavanta was the one who advised Hanumān to fly to Lanka and see Sītā. He was a wise bear and lived through three Yugas. He had a daughter called Jāmbavati and he got the jewel Kaustubha and gave it to her. When Krishna was searching for it, Jāmbavanta fought Krishna and realized that Krishna was none other than Vishnu. He made peace with Vishnu and offered his daughter.

Janaka

Janaka was the king of Mithila. His wife was Ratnamāla and they remained childless for a long time. In order to perform a great sacrifice to have children, Janaka ordered the ground to be ploughed. While ploughing he found a golden box with a small baby girl inside. He took her home and named her Sīta. As Sīta grew she could easily bend the great bow Janaka received from Shiva. He advertised that any prince who could bend the bow would have the hand of Sīta. Many princes tried including Rāvana, but none could bend it. Viswāmitra took Rāma to Mithila and asked Rāma to try bending the bow. Rāma lifted the bow and bent it easily. Knowing that Rāma was the son of Dasaradha, Janaka was pleased and happily allowed Sīta to marry Rāma. His brother Kusadhwaja had three daughters and they were married to the three half-brothers of Rāma. Janaka was an astute king who ruled fairly and justly. His court was home for several Brahmin scholars such as Swetaketu and Yagnavalkya. Owing to his many virtues, Janaka was given Brahminhood before his ascension to the heavens.

Janamējaya

Janamējaya was the son of Parīkshit and great-grandson of Arjuna. The Mahabhārata was told by Vaisampāyana to Janamējaya. His father Parīkshit was killed by the snake Takshaka and when Janamējaya knew this, he started Sarpayagna (snake sacrifice) in which all snakes were fed into the sacrficial fire. The snakes were scared and begged Astika to save them. Astika went to Janamējaya and impressed him with his knowledge and understanding of nature and convinced Janamējaya that snakes were necessary for the ecology and they should be preserved and not killed. After this Janamējaya stopped his sacrifice.

Janārdana

Janārdana was a Brahmin devoted to Vishnu. His friends were Hamsa and Dibhaka. One day Hamsa asked Janardana to go to Krishna and get salt as a tax for him. Janārdana went to Krishna and stayed with him. Krishna later killed Dibhaka and Hamsa using misleading information. (see Hamsa)

Jarāsandha

Jarāsandha was the King of Magadha and the son of Bruhadradha. Bruhadradha was childless for a long time, so he went to the meditating muni Chandakausika and asked to be blessed with a son. The muni took a just fallen fruit, blessed it, and gave it to Bruhadradha suggesting that he should give it to his wife. Bruhadradha had two wives, so he cut the fruit in half and gave one half to each of his wives. They ate it and both became pregnant. When they gave birth the child of each was only half a child with one eye, one ear, and so on as if a complete child split in half. The wives were afraid to show such an ugly half child to Bruhadradha and so threw away the pieces. At that time, a Rākshasi called Jara was passing by and hungry. She saw the two pieces and thought they would make a good meal, so she picked

158

up the child pieces and as she brought them together, they were joined and out came a crying baby boy with enormous strength. Jara was confused and did not know what to do, so she took human form and went to the king and explained what had happened. The king offered food to Jara and took the boy and named him Jarāsandha. When Jarāsnadha came of age, Bruhadradha made him king and retired to the forest.

Jarāsandha became a very powerful king and could not be killed by any weapon. He conquered many weak kings and imprisoned them in his city. He was an ardent worshiper of Bhairava and offered his imprisoned kings as sacrifices. His son-in-law was Kamsa who was killed by Krishna. Krishna thus became his enemy and Jarāsandha went to fight him. Fifteen times he lost and on the sixteenth attempt he won and imprisoned Krishna along with other kings. They all begged Krishna to help them and so he devised a plan. Jarāsandha was a great devotee of Brahma and Brahmins. Any time a Brahmin entered his city, he would personally welcome the guest and offer food and clothes. Krishna appeared as a Brahmin and slipped away to meet with Dharmaja and Bhīma. They all three disguised themselves as Brahmins, entered the city, and were welcomed by Jarāsandha. He greeted them and offered them silk clothes and jewelry and was surprised when they refused to accept his gifts. They then told him that they were not real Brahmins and came actually to fight with him. Jarāsandha told them he was a good king and never harmed them, so why should they come disguised as Brahmins to harm him. Krishna identified himself and said that he had imprisoned many kings unreasonably and was sacrificing them for his own selfish purposes, so they came to kill him.

Jarāsandha said that since they came as guests and their desire was to fight with him, he would fight them and asked what weapons they might need. They told him they did not need any weapons because he could choose any one of them to wrestle. Jarāsnadha agreed to wrestle with Bhīma, and prior to that he installed his son as king. The fight took fourteen days and both sides were knocked down often and it appeared a draw. When Jarāsnadha was down, Krishna signaled Bhīma to finish him off which he did.

Jatāyuvu

Jatāyuvu was a great vulture and brother of Sampāti. One day the two brothers were flying high to see who could fly higher. As they were soaring and reaching the Sun, their feathers were catching fire and Samapāti tried to protect his brother by covering him with his wings. Jatāyuvu was saved, but Sampāti's feathers were burned and he fell to the ocean coast. Jatāyuvu was a good friend of Dasaradha. It was he who rescued Dasaradha and Kausalya from the floods and brought them to Ayodhya. When Rāvana kidnapped Sīta, she cried out loud that she was the wife of Rāma and the daughter-in-law of Dasaradha. Jatāyuvu heard this and came flying to fight Rāvana. He tore Rāvana's chest and arms with his talons, but Rāvana was powerful and chopped Jatāyu's wings. Jatāyuvu fell to the ground and lived until Rāma and Lakshmana passed by. He told them that he was their father's friend and also that Rāvana had kidnapped Sīta. Jatāyuvu then breathed his last. Rāma performed the funeral ritual for him.

Jaya

Jaya was the gatekeeper of Vaikunth, Vishnu's residence. His brother was Vijaya who was also a gatekeeper. When Sanaka, Sananda, and Sanatkumara came to visit Vishnu, the gatekeepers delayed them and they became angry and cursed them to become Rākshasas. Vishnu heard about this and let Jaya and Vijaya come in to explain. Since the curse was irrevocable, Vishnu offered that they could be either his enemies for three lives and return to Vaikunth or his friends for seven lives and return. They chose to be his enemies and thus were Hiranyāksha and Hiranyakasipa, Rāvana and Kumbhakarna, Sisupāla and Danthavaktra.

Jayadradha

Jayadradha was the son of Vruddhakshatra and the King of Sindh. Later in life he took the name Saindhava and fought against the Pāndavas on the side of the Kauravas. He was married to Dussala, daughter of Dhrutarāshtra.

Jayanti

Jayanti was the daughter of Indra. When Sukra was doing great tapas, Indra sent her to disturb him and thus stop him from his tapas. Sukra finished his tapas and received his boons from Brahma and then fell in love with Jayanti. Sukra and Jayanti had a daughter who was Devayāni.

Jīmuthavāhana

Jīmuthavāhana was the son of Jīmuthakethu and the king of Vidyadhara. He was very fond of serving his parents and so often went to the forest where his parents lived. On one of his trips, he saw a beautiful young woman, Malayavati and it was love at first sight and they were married a few days later. Jīmuthavāhana was taken sightseeing by his brother-in-law and on a mountainside he saw a pile of bones. He inquired about the origin of the bones and was told they were the bones of snakes Garuda was eating. When Garuda was killing snakes indiscriminately, a deal was made that everyday one snake would be sent to him as a meal. In return he would kill no more snakes. On that day it was Sankhachuda's turn to become Garuda's meal. He was given the customary red clothes to wear and climb the mountain. At that time Sankhachuda's mother came to bid a last goodbye to her son. Jīmutha saw this and his heart filled with compassion. He offered himself to go and climb the hill. Sankhachuda would not let him do that and while they were arguing, Jīmutha took his wedding dress, which was also red put it on and climbed the hill. Garuda was waiting and began nibbling away at Jīmutha. When he did not return, his parents came searching for him and saw only a few lumps of meat on a skeleton, but recognized it was Jīmutha from the jewelry that had fallen there. By then Sankhachuda also came and begged Garuda to eat him instead, and Garuda realized that he had made a mistake. He went to Indra and asked him to send a nectar shower which Indra did. Suddenly Jīmuthavāhana and all the previously dead serpents came to life. Pārvati was watching all this and was pleased at Jīmuthavāhana's selflessness and good Samaritan hood and she presented him with a gold chariot and blessed him. Thus Jīmuthavāhana became an emperor and ruled Vidyadhara for a long time. Garuda also stopped killing and eating serpents.

Jwara

When Shiva destroyed Daksha's Yagna (special sacrifice), a sweat drop fell from Shiva's forehead and it became an ugly, fierce person and the Devas were afraid of him. Indra begged Shiva to change Jwara into several things and send him to earth to punish unruly earthlings. These things became diseases such as aches, pains, fevers, and anxiety that plagued the earthlings. (fever is Jwara in sanskrit)

Kāveri

Kāveri was a river. Agastya's wife Lopāmudra became the river Kāveri. (see Agastya)

Kabandha

Kabandha was a weird creature that had no head or legs but only a large stomach and enormously long hands. He would twist his arms and eat whatever he could grab. After Sīta was kidnapped, Rāma and Laksmana fell into his hands while searching for her. First they were afraid of this weird creature, but then Rāma cut the hands off and Kabandha died. Just before his death, he asked who they were and when told him they were Rāma and

Lakshmana, he got this shape because of a curse and he would go to heaven if he were cremated. Kabandha also said they should make friends with Sugrīva, who would help them find Sīta.

Kacha

Kacha was the son of Bruhaspati. When the Devas found that Sukra, the rakshasa guru, had the art of reviving the dead (mrutasanjīvi), they sent Kacha to Sukra to learn this. Kacha went to Sukra and became his disciple and also the friend of Sukra's daughter Devayāni. When some rakshasas learned of his intentions they protested with Sukra, but Sukra said Kacha was just another good disciple and favored him. The rakshasas grew jealous and killed Kacha, cremated his body, and mixed the ashes in an alcoholic drink and served it to Sukra. Next day when Kacha was missing, Devayāni asked Sukra to find him. Sukra found out what had happened with his powers and how he had been deceived by his other pupils. He immediately revived Kacha, but Kacha was in his stomach and if he came out Sukra would die. He taught Kacha the art of revival and asked him to come out and revive him, which he did. Since he now knew mrutasanjīvi, Kacha respectfully took leave of Sukra and told Devayāni that he was leaving. Devayāni expressed her love for him and asked him to marry her. Kacha said "you are my guru's daughter and as such you are like my sister, and I cannot marry you". Devayāni became angry and cursed Kacha that the knowledge he learned from her father would not be useful to him. Kacha said "it may not be useful to me, but whomever I teach this to, they will be able to use it. Since you cursed me in anger for no fault of mine, you will not be married to a Brahmin" and left. (see Devayāni)

Kadruva

Kadruva was the daughter of Daksha and Dharani and a wife of Kasyapa. Her children were snakes. One day she and Vinata, another wife of Kasyapa were walking on the beach when they saw the white horse Uchaisrava. Kadruva said to Vinata "what a pity, all of the horse is white except the tail which is black". At that Vinata pointed out that it was not black at all and they argued and bet on the tail being black. If it were black Vinata would become a slave to Kadruva, and if not vice versa. They decided it was too late so they would examine the horse's tail the next day. That night Kadruva called all her children and told them of the bet and begged the big black snake to wind itself around the tail. The next day when they went to examine the tail, it appearred to be black and so Vinata became a servant of Kadruva. Vinata had a son called Garuda who freed her of the slavery to Kadruva by bringing nectar from Indra. (see Garuda)

Aditi came to Kasyapa to have sex and saw him with Kadruva. She became angry and cursed them to become humans and Kadruva counter-cursed her. Kasyapa became Vasudeva, Aditi became Devaki, and Kadruva became Rohini.

Kālanemi

Kālanemi was the son of Marichi and a friend of Rāvana. His daughter was Brunda, who married Jalandhara. When Hanumān was bringing Sanjīvi to revive Laksmana, Rāvana asked Kālanemi to kill Hanumān. Kālanemi disguised as a rishi, asked Hanumān to bathe in the lake nearby and his wishes would be fulfilled. The lake was filled with crocodiles and serpents and he assumed Hanumān would be killed. Hanumān came out unscathed and killed Kālanemi. In the next life Kālanemi would come as Kamsa.

Kāli

Kāli was a great Devi called Chandika. She was angry at the demons and from her face blackened with anger came Kāli with a sword and tiger skin clothes. She had a third eye which could burn anything to ashes. She killed many demons and when she saw Shiva, she fell in love with him and asked him to marry her. Shiva asked for the third eye which she promptly gave him, but Shiva still refused her. She remained an angry Goddess.

Kāliya

Kāliya was a snake son of Kadruva and a ferocious serpent. He was not sharing offerings with Garuda and after a fight fled to a lake called Kālindi where he poisoned the whole lake with his venom. Even birds flying above the lake died from the venom. Many innocent lives were consumed by Kāliya. One day Krishna jumped into the lake from a tree and landed on Kāliya's head and began to dance. Kāliya tried to bite him but could not. Slowly he grew tired and weak. All of Kāliya's wives prayed to Krishna to spare his life and prevent them from becoming widows. Krishna took pity on them and asked Kāliya to leave the lake and go to the netherworld where Garuda could not harm him.

Kamsa

Kamsa was the son of Ugrasena. One day Ugrasena's wife went swimming with a few of her friends and she had her period. She had romantic feelings and thought of her husband. However, a demon called Dravila was watching all this and assumed the likeness of Ugrasena and had sex with her. When she found out that it was not her husband, she asked him who he was. When told that he was the demon Dravila, she cursed him that his son would be killed by an incarnation of Vishnu. That son was Kamsa and he had all the traits of the demons. He married the daughter of Jarāsandha and his friends were Sisupāla, Pūtana, and other demons. He imprisoned his father and assumed the throne. He was told by Nārada that he would be killed by the eighth son of Devaki and Vasudeva. Devaki was his cousin *(sister)* and he wanted to kill her. She begged him and promised that she would give him all her babies immediately after they were born, so he could kill them. Kamsa put both Devaki and Vasudeva in prison and was killing each of their children soon after their birth. Vasudeva took the eighth son to the next village and exchanged him with a baby girl born to Yasoda. The next day Kamsa took the baby girl and was about to kill her when she vanished and a voice from the heavens told Kamsa that a boy growing with Yasoda would kill him. The boy was none other than Krishna. Kamsa sent many demons to trick and kill Krishna, but was not successful. He sent Pūtana to go to Krishna and give him poisoned milk from her breast. Krishna knew that and sucked the life out of her. Finally Krishna faced Kamsa and killed him in a fight. Kamsa was Kālanemi in a previous life.

Kanva

Kanva was a great muni and a descendent of Kasyapa. One day he saw a small girl being protected from the Sun by birds spreading their wings. He took the girl home and named her Sakuntala. Sakuntala grew up to be a very beautiful woman and when King Dushyanta visited Kanva's ashram, he fell in love with Sakuntala and they were happy together. Sakuntala was soon pregnant and was afraid that Kanva would be angry. Kanva approved of the affair and she gave birth to a son Bharata. As the boy grew and became a powerful man, Kanva sent Bharata and Sakuntala to Dushyanta who first refused to acknowledge the affair. A voice from the heavens confirmed that Bharata was indeed his son and he would become a great king. (see Bharata)

Kapila

Kapila was a great muni and the son of Devahūti and Kardama. Kapila was meditating when the sons of Sagara found their sacrificial horse next to Kapila. They thought Kapila had stolen their horse and was about to kill him when he destroyed them all. It was much later Bhagīratha, the grandson of Sagara prayed to Ganga and brought her to flow over the ashes of his uncles so they could go to the heavens. Actually the horse was planted there by Indra who stole it to disturb Sagara's sacrifice. Kapila was the author of Sankhya Upanishad.

Kardama

Kardama was one of the great rishis and also a Prajāpati. He was praying to Vishnu and soon Vishnu appeared to grant him a wish. Kardama asked to have children and was granted this wish provided he found a wife. He asked for the hand of Devahūti, the daughter of Swāyambhuva Manu. They had nine daughters including Anasūya and Arundhati. When Kardama wanted to become a sanyasi, Devahūti asked him for a son first and then he would become a sanyasi. That son was Kapila.

Karna

Karna was the son of Kunti and the Sun. When Kunti served Dūrvāsa, he was so pleased he gave her a mantra. With the mantra she could call any god and ask for a son by him. She was eager to test this power and called for the Sun. When the Sun appeared, she asked for a son like him. That was Karna and as she was still unmarried and afraid of scandals, Kunti put Karna in a basket and sent it down the river. Karna was picked up by Sūta, a charioteer who was childless and was brought up in his house. He was a powerful and gifted archer who studied under Parasurāma. His rivalry with Arjuna was formidable. When he wanted to attempt the fish machine for the hand of Draupadi, he was denied the opportunity because he was not of noble birth. Duryodhana made him viceroy and offered his friendship. Since then, Karna faithfully served Duryodhana and finally became commander-in-chief after Bhīshma and Drōna in the Great War.

Karna was a great giver; he never refused a request. In order to help his son Arjuna, Indra disguised himself as a Brahmin. He went to Karna and asked him for his natural armor. Karna immediately peeled it off and gave it away. Karna asked him why a Brahmin would need the armor. Indra then assumed his form and told the truth that he wanted to help Arjuna, and Karna could not be killed as long as he had his armor. He admired Karna and gave him a special weapon that would kill anyone. Eventually Karna had to use that weapon against Ghatotkacha.

After twelve years in the forests and one-year incognito, the Pāndavas sent Krishna to negotiate their share of the kingdom and avoid war. During those negotiations, Bhīshma and Drōna advised Duryodhana to yield and give them their share and keep peace. Karna objected to this and advised Duryodhana not to concede. There was a great argument between Karna and Bhīshma in which Bhīshma belittled Karna by telling him that he was an Ardharadha (half a charioteer). An offended Karna vowed to not take up arms as long as Bhīshma was the commander. Karna went to Parasurāma and asked him to teach the use of the special weapon Pasupata. Parasurāma said he would teach the weapon only for warriors of Brahmin origin. Karna pretended he was a Brahmin and learned the use of Pasupata. One day Parasurāma was resting using Karna's lap as a pillow, and Indra saw the opportunity to betray Karna. He came as a worm and bored through Karna's thigh. Karna endured the pain rather than waking up his guru. At the feel of warm blood, Parasurāma woke up and asked what had happened. When Karna explained, Parasurāma suspected that Karna was not a Brahmin because Brahmins do not have such ability for endurance, and asked for the truth. When told the truth, he became angry and cursed

Karna that he would not remember the weapon's use just when he needed it.

After the failed negotiations, Krishna approached Karna secretly and told him that he really was Kunti's firstborn son and he should consider switching sides and fight with the Pāndavas. Karna politely refused saying that although he had heard of such rumors, he really could not consider abandoning Duryodhana who had given him all the rights and privileges of a king. One day when he was performing rituals in the river, Kunti approached him and told him who he really was. She too asked him to join the Pāndavas and become the sixth Pāndava. He respectfully bowed to her, and said "oh mother there are only five Pāndavas not six. Also my rivalry with Arjuna has to be settled in a battle, otherwise people would think I was a coward. The battle will go on and I will not harm any of the other four. If I win, I will certainly take my position as a Pāndava. I know it is not going to be, because there are too many curses on me and I gave my natural armor away".

When the war came, Drōna became the commander shortly after Bhīshma. Karna fought alongside Bhīshma. He defeated Dharmaja, Bhīma, Nakula, and Sahadeva, but never killed them although he could have. Finally after Drōna, Karna himself became the commander. He asked for a good charioteer because Krishna was the charioteer for Arjuna. Only Salya was of this caliber, so Duryodhana went to Salya and begged him to become Karna's charioteer. Salya became angry at the request, but finally agreed although his sympathies were with the Pāndavas. In the battle, he would discourage Karna by telling him that he had a poor aim and so on. As the final battle was taking place, Karna suddenly forgot the procedure for Pasupata and at the same time his chariot sank into the ground because of a curse. He got down and tried to lift the chariot wheel, the earth shook but the wheel did not come loose. At that moment Krishna urged Arjuna to finish him off even though Karna was on the ground and had no bow and arrow in his hand. Arjuna followed Krishna's advice and felled him with a powerful arrow.

Karna was Sahasrakavacha (thousand armored one) in a previous life. Nara and Nārayana could penetrate and destroy all of them except one. Karna was born with the last remaining one and to kill him Nara and Nārayana came as Arjuna and Krishna.

Kasyapa

Kasyapa was the son of Maricha and the adopted son of the Sun. Longing to have children (sons), Kasyapa drank raw fermented brew (wine). Daksha became angry with Kasyapa for drinking and cursed him. When Kasyapa was about to counter-curse, Brahma appeared and ordered Daksha to give his daughters in marriage to Kasyapa. Among those were Diti, Aditi, Vinata, and Karduva. All the Devas, Danavas (demons), Naras (men and women), animals, and trees were all his offspring. Kasyapa is also one of the Prajāpatis.

When Aditi wanted to make love and approached Kasyapa, she found him with Kadruva. In a jealous rage she cursed them to be born as humans. Kasyapa became Vasudeva and Aditi was born as Devaki.(see Kadruva) Many of Vishnu's incarnations are

Kasyapa's offspring, Vāmana, Rāma, and Krishna.

Kasyapa (2)

Kasyapa was a renowned Brahmin and an expert in poisons. When he heard that Parīkshit would be destroyed by the snake Takshaka, he was going to rescue the king. Takshaka met him on the way and asked him where he was going and why. He replied that he was going to rescue the king and earn some riches for his act. Takshaka laughed and said "no one could restore what I can destroy" and thus an argument ensued. Takshaka challenged him and bit a tree. The tree was dead along with all the creatures in it. Kasyapa used his skill and restored the tree and all the life in it. Then Takshaka offered Kasyapa many riches and asked him to return to his village, so he could go and accomplish his mission of destroying Parīkshit.

Kausalya

Kausalya was the daughter of Bhānumanta, King of Kosala. One day when she was taking a stroll in the royal gardens, she met Dasaradha and fell in love with him. Her father gave permission for them to marry and as their entourage camped on a riverbank, a huge flash flood washed them away. Rāvana heard that he would be killed by the son of Kausalya, so he kidnapped her and wanted to kill her. Nārada appeared and advised Rāvana not to kill Kausalya but wait for her son. Rāvana put her in a box and drowned her in the river. Down the river, Dasaradha saw the box in which Kausalya was floating, and retrieved her. They were married immediately in the presence of Jatāyuvu, who took them

173

later to Ayodhya. For a long time the couple had no children and after Dasaradha performed a great sacrifice, Kausalya gave birth to a son and that was Rāma. (see Dasaradha) In a previous life, Dasaradha was Kasyapa and Kausalya was Aditi.

Kausika

Kausika was a Brahmin seeking knowledge by meditation under a tree. One day a bird dropping fell on him and he looked up angrily at the bird, and the bird was annihilated. He was amazed at his powers, and went begging for food. When he approached a house and asked for some food, the woman of the house did not hasten to please him. This angered him and he demanded an explanation. She replied that she was serving her husband and for married women husbands come first. She also said "your anger might have destroyed the bird, but it has no effect on me". He was surprised how she knew about the bird, and asked her how she knew of it. She replied that she was a strict adherer of duties and she served her husband all the time, and through that power she knew what went on. She taught him some Dharma and suggested that he should go and see Dharmavyādha, a butcher in the city of Mithila. When Kausika went to Dharmavyādha, he knew about him and offered his hospitality. Kausika was surprised again and asked him how a butcher like him knew about Dharma. The butcher explained that it was his duty and if he did not discharge his duties, it would be wrong. He took Kausika to his home and introduced him to his parents and explained that his knowledge comes from them. He also suggested that Kausika should go home and serve his aging parents first and then seek the knowledge.

174

Dharmavyādha was a Brahmin in a previous life. He was very skilled with bow and arrow and had many princes among his circle of friends. Once when he was hunting, he shot a hermit by mistake and was cursed by the hermit to be born as a butcher.

Ketu

Ketu was a friend of Rāhu who received the nectar and became immortal. Both were demons focused on tormenting the Sun and Moon and causing eclipses.

Kīchaka

Kīchaka was the brother-in-law of King Virāta and also known as Simhabala (lion-strong). When he was visiting his sister Sudheshna, he saw Draupadi there and fell in love with her. He made advances to Draupadi and when she refused, he threatened to rape her. Draupadi complained to Bhīma of Kīchaka's advances and they plotted to eliminate Kīchaka. When Kīchaka tried the next day, Draupadi pretended to be agreeing and asked him to meet her in the royal gardens that night when it would be dark. In the meantime Bhīma dressed as a woman was waiting for Kīchaka. When he finally came expecting the warm embrace of Draupadi, it was Bhīma who embraced him and crushed him to death.

Bhīma, Kīchaka, and Duryodhana were all of equal strength. Whoever killed one first, the other would die at the hands of the first one. Duryodhana was also killed by Bhīma.

Kishkindha

Kishkindha was a region of the country on the banks of the river Pampa and was ruled by Vāli and Sugrīva.

Krishna

Krishna was the eighth incarnation of Vishnu. Born as the eighth child of Devaki and Vasudeva, Krishna was to kill his uncle Kamsa. Kamsa imprisoned Devaki and ordered the guards to bring the newborn children of Devaki right away. When Krishna was born, the guards fell asleep and Vasudeva took the child, crossed the river, and put the baby next to Yasoda who had given birth to a girl at the same time. He brought the baby girl and handed her over to the guards. When Kamsa was about to kill the child, it disappeared invoking a voice that said "a child who is going to kill you is growing with Yasoda in the next village". Kamsa was afraid and determined to kill that child any way he could. Although the child was born fair-skinned, when he was put next to Yasoda he became dark-skinned and hence the name Krishna (meaning dark one).

Determined to kill Krishna by any means, Kamsa gathered several Rākshasas and sent them in different forms to kill Krishna. First came Trunavarta in the form of a twister and lifted Krishna off the ground, but Krishna became very heavy and dragged the demon to earth and killed him. Next came Pūtana in the form of a young mother who liked Krishna so much she offered to breastfeed him with poison milk. Krishna knew of this trick and he sucked not just milk but the whole life out of her until she fell dead. Many others followed in different forms and they all met the same fate.

Krishna was a very mischievous child. He would steal butter and milk from the farmers and give it to monkeys and other children. When it was too much Yasoda tied him to a roller, but Krishna crawled and when the roller was stuck between two trees, he pulled the trees down and out came two hermits who blessed Krishna and left. One day the other children complained to Yasoda that Krishna was eating dirt. Yasoda confronted him and asked if it were true. Krishna opened his mouth and Yasoda saw the whole universe in his mouth and knew her son was not an ordinary little boy. Although he was extraordinary, Krishna easily mingled with his playmates and took the cows every day to the

178

meadows for grazing. One day on their return from the meadows, the cows drank water from a nearby lake called Kālindi and died. The lake was infested with poison from the great snake Kāliya. Krishna revived the cows and climbed a tree and landed on the head of Kāliya and began stomping. Kāliya could not bite him and was getting very weak with his head being bashed. His wives came and prayed to Krishna and begged him not to make them widows. Krishna took pity, got down, and ordered Kāliya to go to the netherworld and not be mean and poisonous.

One day Brahma hid the cows and the cowherds in a cave to test Krishna. Krishna looked everywhere and did not find the cows and was puzzled what to say to the villagers about their children and their cows. He took the shapes of the children and cows and went to each home as if nothing had happened. Brahma was surprised and pleased and let the cows and the cowherds free. Krishna's childhood deeds were impossible to describe. Once when Nanda (Yasoda's husband) was preparing for a large sacrifice to Indra, Krishna said if Nanda wanted, he should please the Brahmins, cows, rivers and the mountains and not Indra because he had everything. Indra became angry and began raining stones to hurt the villagers and Nanda. Krishna lifted the mountain Govardhana with his finger and led all the villagers and cows under it to protect them from the hale of stones. Indra was ashamed and begged Krishna for forgiveness.

Krishna grew to be handsome and mighty so all the Gopikas (herd women) fell in love with him. Krishna played the flute and when he played all the cows, Gopikas, and bystanders stood still in admiration. One day the Gopikas went to the river, took off their

179

clothes and began swimming. Krishna saw this, sneaked up and stole their clothes. He climbed a tree and began playing his flute. The Gopikas heard and looked up to find him with their clothes. They begged him to give back their clothes, and to that he said to simply come out and get them. When they hesitated and were shy, he reminded them there was nothing he did not know so it was all right for them to come out and get their clothes.

Krishna's fame was heard of far and wide, even by Kamsa. Kamsa tried many tricks to kill Krishna. He invited Krishna and his brother Balarāma to his city and ordered poisoned garlands to be offered to them. The trick was easily detected and the garlands were offered to Kamsa's lieutenants and they were killed instead. Kamsa tried to stomp the hut where Krishna was staying with drunken elephants. That too was neutralized when the mahouts were killed and the elephants turned round to trample Kamsa's city instead. Kamsa finally faced Krishna and was killed by him. After that Krishna freed his real parents Devaki and Vasudeva. Jarāsandha was Kamsa's uncle. He heard of the demise of his nephew and so was in search of Krishna. Krishna accompanied by Arjuna and Bhīma went to Jarāsandha, challenged him to a fight and in that fight Bhīma killed him.(see Jarāsandha)

Krishna married Rukmini, daughter of Bhīmasena. Rukmini's brother wanted her to marry Sisupāla who was also a friend of Kamsa and Jarāsandha. When the day of the husband search came, Rukmini secretly sent word to Krishna that he should come and kidnap her, which he did. When the others were following him to fight he defeated them all and went to Dwāraka with Rukmini. In addition to Rukmini, Krishna married many others including Rādha, all in all some sixteen thousand Gopikas.

Satrajit obtained a special jewel called Syamantaka from the Sun, and refused to give it to Krishna when he asked for it. A few days later Prasena, Satrajit's brother wore the jewel and went hunting. He was attacked and killed by a lion that took the jewel from him. Jāmbavanta killed the lion and took the jewel Syamantaka and gave it to his daughter. Satrajit accused Krishna of killing his brother and stealing the jewel. Krishna went searching and found Jāmbavanta's daughter with the jewel and tried to take it away from her. At that moment Jāmbavanta came in and fought with Krishna. Jāmbavanta was a very strong bear king and was surprised that Krishna was not defeated. Finally he recognized who Krishna was, apologized and gave both his daughter and the jewel to Krishna. When Krishna returned the jewel to Satrajit, he was ashamed for accusing Krishna wrongfully, so he too apologized and gave his daughter Satyabhāma along with the jewel to Krishna. Once Indra came to Krishna and told him that Naraka stole Aditi's jewels. Krishna went with Satyabhāma to Naraka and with her help killed Naraka. That day was the day before the new moon in October, and because Naraka was such a vicious demon, his death was celebrated with lights. This event is celebrated as the festival of lights (Divali).

Krishna attended Draupadi's swayamvara not to compete, but only to participate. There he met the Pāndavas and became very friendly with Arjuna. Krishna took him to Dwāraka and married off his sister Subhadra to Arjuna. They were always together and on one occasion Agni came and asked for their help in consuming the gardens of Khāndava. For that help Agni rewarded them with the great bow Gāndiva for Arjuna and the Chakra for Krishna.

181

Many kings were jealous and afraid of Krishna, one of them was Sālva. He was creating illusions and harassing Krishna's people. He even attempted to deceive Krishna by creating a false Vasudeva and crying out loud that he was going to kill Vasudeva. Krishna knew of these tricks and so at the right moment he sent his Chakra to cut Sālva's head off.

While Krishna was engaged in small skirmishes with jealous neighbor kings, he could not visit the Pāndavas. By the time he could inquire about them, it was too late. They lost all their wealth to Duryodhna and had to go to the forests. Krishna went to visit them in the forest. At the same time Dūrvāsa wanted to embarrass them and so descended upon them with an entourage of a hundred Brahmins. Draupadi did not have anything to cook to feed them. Krishna saw this and asked her to show him the pot in which she wanted to cook. There was a single rice particle and Krishna took it and ate it. Immediately that pot became full with rice and could not be emptied. Thus Draupadi could feed all of the guests. That pot was Akshayapātra.

At the end of the year of incognito of the Pāndavas, Krishna tried to act as a mediator between the Kauravas and the Pāndavas to prevent the war, but with no success. Krishna became the charioteer for Arjuna and on the first day of the battle Arjuna wanted to examine the Kaurava armies. When he saw that all of the enemies were his cousins, gurus, and great uncles, he wanted to renounce the weapons. Krishna taught him Bhagavadgītā, the song of the gods. Krishna saved the life of Arjuna twice in the battle with Karna. When the Pāndavas won the war, Duryodhna disappeared and hid in the ocean. Krishna challenged him to come out and fight with Bhīma, and he signaled Bhīma to hit Duryodhana on the thighs to kill him.

Krishna had several children with his many wives, but they all perished very young due to quarrels and betrayals among themselves. The people of Dwāraka had also become complacent and begun to lead frivolous lives with too many quarrels and too many killings. Disgusted with all this Balarāma went to the mountains and Krishna was going to visit him. On the way he was resting under a tree when a hunter mistook him for an animal and shot an arrow through his feet killing him. In the previous incarnation as Rāma, Krishna killed Vāli from behind without any justifiable reason. That is why Krishna was killed by the hunter who was the incarnation of Vāli's son Angada, also without reason. Arjuna went searching for Krishna and found his body and performed the final rituals for Krishna.

Krishnadwaipāyana

Krishnadwaipāyana was a great rishi from the beginning of time and also known as Vyāsa. He was born as the son of Parāsara and Satyavati and expanded the Vedas and became Vedavyāsa. Among his disciples were Sanjaya, Vaisampāyana, Sumanta, and Jaimini. He sent Vaisampāyana to tell the story of Mahabhārta to Janamējaya, the great grandson of Arjuna. (see Vyāsa)

Krupa and Krupi

Krupa and Krupi were the son and daughter of Saradvanta. Indra wanted to destroy Sardvanta's meditation and so sent an apsara to distract him. When Saradvanta saw the apsara, he ejaculated and the sperm fell into two parts and became a boy and girl. One day when Santana was hunting he found the two children, took pity upon them, and took them to his palace. The children were given the names Krupa and Krupi, meaning mercy. Krupi married Drōna and their son was Aswatthāma. Krupa became a general and advisor to Duryodhana.

Kubera

Kubera was the Son of Pulastya and the ruler of the North. His half-brother was Rāvana. He prayed to Brahma and received several boons including control of wealth and the city/state called Lanka. Kubera also received the flying chariot, Pushpaka. Pulastya was angered by Kubera for his prayers to Brahma, so he created Visrāvasu and ordered him to take away Kubera's wealth. After hearing this, Kubera went to Visrāvasu and asked if he could become his son and serve him, which he did. During this time Visrāvasu found three women Pushpotkata, Mālini, and Pāka and married them. Pushpotkata gave birth to Rāvana and Kumbhakarna. Rāvana prayed to Shiva and made enormous sacrifices and got several boons. When he returned from his tapas, he asked Kubera to leave Lanka. When Kubera protested, he banished him from Lanka. Kubera went to Kailas and prayed to Shiva who gave him his friendship and a city called Alaka and made him the ruler of the North. One day when Shiva and Pārvati were relaxing, Kubera looked at Pārvati with a jealous eye and his right eye popped immediately. Kubera begged Shiva to pardon him, and he was pardoned and his eye was restored. When Kubera heard that Rāvana was ruling Lanka unfairly, he sent a messenger pleading with Rāvana to behave in a righteous manner. Rāvana killed the messenger, attacked Kubera, defeated him, and took the Pushpaka. It was this flying chariot that Rāma used to return to Ayodhya after killing Rāvana and later returned it to Kubera.

Kuchela

Kuchela was a poor Brahmin who was a classmate of Krishna. He had lots of children but not the means to feed them. His wife asked him to go to Krishna and ask him for help. She packed some flat rice for Krishna because that was all she had in the house. Kuchela went to Dwāraka and was not sure whether Krishna would even receive him. To his surprise, Krishna was waiting for him and they reminisced about their youth and Krishna ate the rice gladly. After a few days of staying with Krishna, Kuchela left without asking for anything and Krishna did not offer anything either. Kuchela thought this was good because if he were given wealth, he would be obssessed by the wealth and neglect his friend Krishna. As he approached his hut he could not believe what he saw. His house was transformed into a castle with all of the pomp and pleasures. Kuchela knew how it all came about, and he became an ardent follower of Krishna.

Kumāraswami

Kumāraswami was the son of Shiva and Pārvati. Indra was jealous that the son of Shiva and Pārvati would be greater and more powerful than he, so he asked Agni to prevent that child from being born. While Shiva and Pārvati were making love, Agni suddenly appeared before them. Pārvati was angry and dumped the sperm on Agni. Agni was grievously upset by this and then asked Ganga to carry Shiva's sperm. Ganga said yes, but soon did not want to be burdened with it, so she hid it in the sawgrass. Thus was born the child Kumāraswami who was made leader of the heavenly armies. He rode a Peacock.

Agni was lusting for the wives of several rishis. His wife Swaha discovered this and assumed the form of each wife except Arundhati (wife of Vasishta) and made love with Agni. Each time she took the sperm and preserved it. The newborn child had six faces and was very powerful. Brahma welcomed the child into the heavens and explained how he was born and for what purpose. He made him the leader of the heavenly armies. Kumāraswami is also known as Kārtikeya and Skanda.

Kumbhakarna

Kumbhakarna was the brother of Rāvana and a very powerful man. Along with Rāvana, Kumbhakarna made great sacrifices and tapas. The Devas were very upset about this and complained to Brahma about Kumbhakarna's strength, insisting that he would destroy the world if he acquired more. Brahma sent his wife

Saraswati to make Kumbhakarna say sleep, which rhymed with no-mercy (Nidra instead of Nirdaya) as his desire. When this happened, Kumbhakarna was saddened because all of his sacrifices amounted to nothing. His father Visrāvasu complained to Brahma that he had been cheated and the boon should be reversed. Brahma said that would not be possible, but when Kumbhakarna was awake he would be undefeatable and he would be weakened if he were awakened before he naturally got up. Kumbhakarna would be awake naturally only one day every six months. Rāvana built a special castle for him so he would not be disturbed while sleeping. When the war with Rāma came, Kumbhakarna was awakened and during the fighting he was killed by Lakshmana.

Kunti

Kunti was the mother of Dharmaja, Arjuna, Karna, Bhīma, and the Pāndavas.

Lakshmana

Lakshmana was the son of Dasaradha and Sumitra and the half-brother of Rāma. Lakshmana and Rāma grew up together. They completed their studies and learned martial arts together. As the boys grew and were becoming young men, the great Viswāmitra came and asked Dasaradha if the two boys could come with him to destroy some demons. Dasaradha first hesitated because he felt the boys were too young, but finally agreed to send them with

Viswāmitra. Viswāmitra performed his ritual without any disturbances from the demons especially Māricha and Subāha, and then took them to the city of Mithila ruled by King Janaka. Janaka had a daughter Sīta who was married to Rāma. Lakshmana married Urmila, a cousin of Sīta. When Rāma was ordered to go to the forests, Lakshmana argued with his father and even threatened to crown Rāma with his own strength i.e. fighting with the father. Lakshmana was very dedicated to Rāma. In the end, he followed Rāma and Sīta to the forest leaving behind all the royal comforts and even his new bride.

They crossed many rivers including the Ganga and visited many rishis, one of whom was Bharadwāja. While they were with him, they saw Bharata coming with his entourage. Lakshmana thought Bhrata was coming to fight and so asked Rāma to get ready, but when Bharata approached he prostrated at Rāma's feet. He gave him the bad news that their father Dasaradha had passed away and begged Rāma to come back to Ayodhya and rule. Rāma said there is no way for him to renege on his promise to their father, and he would return only after completing the fourteen years of forest life. Bharata took Rāma's sandals and crowned them in a coronation ceremony. Rāma and Lakshmana set up a bamboo hut and Lakshmana was keeping watch during the nights pacing up and down with his bow stretched. One day Sūrpanakha, a sister of Rāvana came by and fell in love with Rāma. When he refused her, she asked Laksmana to marry her. When he too refused her, she became angry and began cursing them. At that point Lakshmana seized her and cut her nose and ears. Screaming, she went away and vowed revenge.

Soon Māricha came as a golden deer and Sītā wanted it. Lakshmana dismissed it as a trick, but Rāma went chasing it anyway. A few minutes later, they heard a shriek "Oh Lakshmana help" and Sītā thought Rāma was hurt and asked Lakshmana to go and help him. Lakshmana said it was all some kind of trick, and she should not be worried. Sītā got angry and accused him of bad intentions. Lakshmana drew a line and asked Sītā not to cross it for any reason and went to see Rāma. While he was gone, Rāvana came and stole Sītā. When they returned, the hut was empty and they began searching for Sītā. On their way they saw Jatāyuvu who told them that Rāvana had kidnapped Sītā. They also saw Kabandha and killed him, but first learned from him that they should go to Kishkindha and make friends with Sugrīva who would help them find Sītā. They went to Kishkindha and killed Vāli and made Sugrīva the monkey king. After that Sugrīva sent his search team to find Sītā and they returned with the news that she was in captivity in Lanka. Sugrīva assembled a great army of monkeys and bears and went to conquer Rāvana and bring back Sītā. During the fight, Rāvana's son Indrajit stunned Lakshmana, and Hanumān had to get the medicine Sanjīva to revive Lakshmana. In that fight Lakshmana killed Kumbhakarna. Finally they all returned to Ayodhya and Rāma reigned for a long time. The gods felt it was time for Vishnu to end the incarnation of Rāma and get back to Vaikunth, the heavenly abode of Vishnu. In a court session, a lower class man who had just divorced his wife made a derogatory remark about Rāma and Sītā. Hearing the remark, Rāma decided to abandon Sītā and asked Lakshmana to take her and leave her in the forest. He did it with a great grief and at the moment he would be leaving Sītā behind, he was very sad. Sītā comforted him and said she knew of Rāma abandoning her and she would somehow survive and raise the children of

Rāma, because she was pregnant.

One day Yama came as a Brahmin and asked for a private audience with Rāma. Rāma granted the audience and posted Lakshmana at the gate to see that no one would enter the chamber, and if someone did that person would lose his head. Dūrvāsa came and asked to be let in. When Lakshmana refused, Dūrvāsa taunted him "how can you stop a hungry Brahmin from going inside the house to get a bite and a sip of water? What kind of royalty is this?" Lakshmana went in to see if it was all right. As soon as he entered, Yama disappeared and Rāma was surprised. True to his word Rāma was about to sever Lakshmana's head, then Dūrvāsa came in and urged Rāma to banish Lakshmana into exile instead of killing him because exile for life is equal to killing. Thus banished, Lakshmana was crossing the river Sarayu and drowned.

Lakshmi

Lakshmi was the wife of Vishnu. Owing to a curse by Dūrvāsa, she was hiding in the ocean. When the ocean was churned, she came out again and joined Vishnu. She was also reincarnated with Vishnu; when Vishnu came as Rāma she came as Sīta, for Krishna she came as Rukmini.

Lanka

Lanka was an island off the coast of Jambūdvīpa (India) formed as

190

a result of a contest between Vāyu and the original serpent Adisesha. In order to test their strength, Adisesha bound himself to the mountain Mēru, and Vāyu blew as hard as he could to separate them. Instead of separating Mēru from Adisesha, he ripped off the top of Mēru and it landed in the ocean forming Lanka. Brahma came to Lanka to meditate and to disturb him Indra sent Urvasi. When Brahma saw Urvasi, he ejaculated and thus was born Pulastya, whose grandson was Rāvana who later ruled Lanka.

Lata

Lata was one of the Apsaras. She once came to earth to disturb a Brahmin from his tapas, and was cursed to become an alligator. When Lata begged for mercy, she was told that whenever she was taken out of water, she would become an apsara again. When Arjuna was bathing in the river during one of his pilgrimages, he encountered the alligator Lata. He took hold of the alligator and threw it out of the water. The animal became a woman again and went to the heavens.

Lingam

Many rishis were performing great tapas for the good of mankind, and Shiva came to test them. He was appearing in many forms, making different noises, and even streaking by without clothes. The rishis were annoyed and ordered Shiva to wear clothes and not disturb them, otherwise his penis would drop off. Shiva hid his body and appeared only as Lingam and stopped creation. The rishis then went to Brahma and begged for relief. Knowing Lingam was none other than Shiva himself, Brahma ordered that Shiva should be respected and worshiped only in the form of Lingam. This is why Shiva temples have only Lingam as the statue form of worship.

Lohitāsya

Lohitāsya was the son of Harischandra and Chandramati. In order to keep his word, Harischandra lost his wealth and even had to sell his wife as a slave. One day while Lohitāsya was gathering twigs for a fire, he was bitten by a snake and died. Chandramati brought him to the burial site where Harschandra was the site keeper. They recognized each other, but Chandramati had to come up with the burial tax. While she was trying to get it, some thieves dropped stolen jewelry in her bag and she was falsely accused and convicted. It was the duty of Harischandra to perform the beheading. At that time Viswāmitra and other rishis appeared, praised Harischandra, and revived Lohitāsya and gave their kingdom back to them. (see Harischandra and Chandramati)

Lopāmudra

Lopāmudra was the wife of Agastya and the daughter of Kavera. (see Kāveri and Agastya)

Mādri

Mādri was the wife of Pāndu and the mother of Nakula and Sahadeva. Pāndu had been cursed that he would die when he made love to his wives. Kunti through her ability to invoke any god had three children with Yama, Indra, and Vāyu. Lending her ability to Mādri gave Madri two sons from Aswini Devas. Soon after this Pāndu could not resist the beauty of Mādri and he made love to her and immediately died. Mādri followed him throwing herself on the funeral pyre. Kunti raised Mādri's sons.

Māndavya

Māndavya was a great hermit who invented the ability to conquer desire, but he himself was suffering from a wound. Once Kausika's wife was carrying him on her shoulder and his toe touched Māndavya and his wound was scratched. Shrieking from pain, he cursed the person who had caused the pain to die before sunrise. Being a great Pativrata, Kausika's wife ordered the Sun not to rise. When everybody was feeling the misery for not having the Sun, Anasūya approached Kausika's wife and asked her to rescind her order to the Sun and she would bring her husband back to life. (see Anasūya and Kausika)

Māndavya went to Yama and asked why he was punished in this way. Yama told him that as a boy he caught butterflies and killed them, so he was being punished for these actions. Māndavya protested that although he deserved some punishment, what he got was cruel and out of proportion to his crime. He cursed Yama

193

to be born as a human to a lower class woman. That was Vidura, half-brother of Dhrutarāshtra and Pāndu.

Māndhata

Māndhata was the son of Yuvanēswa. He was powerful and became king at the age of twelve. Māndhata conquered all of the earth and declared war against Indra, but was cheated out of the victory. Rāvana heard of Māndhata and asked him for a fight in which Māndhata defeated Rāvana and chained him. Brahma then intervened and restored peace between them. They remained friends from then on. Māndhata was considered the greatest king of Krutayuga (the first period).

Māricha

Māricha was the son of Tātaka. He and his brother Subāha were destroying the sacrifice of Viswāmitra. Viswāmitra took Rāma and Lakshmana to save his sacrifice by throwing them out. Māricha took his revenge for this by appearing as a golden deer and distracting Rāma so that Rāvana could kidnap Sīta.

Mārkandeya

Mārkandeya was one of the great rishis who conquered death. He was the son of Mrukandu and Manaswini. When he was twelve years old, he was dragged by Yama *(god of death)*. Mārkandeya prayed to Shiva by hugging a lingam and not paying any attention to anything. When Yama tried to pull him, Shiva intervened and asked Yama to leave Mārkandeya alone because from then on he would not die. Mārkandeya was one of the greatest rishis and he was above the tricks of Indra. When the world was flooded, Mārkandeya was one of the few who survived and saw Vishnu sleeping on a banyan leaf and witnessed creation again. Mārkandeya roamed the earth through the Yugas, visited the Pāndavas and taught dharma to Dharmaja.

Mārtanda

Mārtand was an incarnation of Sun. When the Devas were short-changed by the Daityas, they prayed to Aditi to save them. She in turn prayed to the Sun who told her he would be born as her son. Aditi was fasting when pregnant with Mārtanda, and her husband Kasyapa asked her to stop fasting otherwise she would kill the fetus. Aditi became angry and gave birth to a boy who was so powerful he scorched his enemies right away. That boy was Mārtanda, one of the Suns.

Māyavi

Māyavi was the son of Maya and brother of Dundubhi. When Vāli killed Dundubhi, Māyavi went to Kishkindha at night and challenged Vāli to come and fight with him. As they were fighting fiercely, Māyavi ran into a cave and Vāli followed him and they fought in the cave. After a long fight, blood began to flow from the cave. Vāli's brother Sugrīva thought Vāli was dead and so closed the cave with a huge boulder. Vāli with his enormous strength pushed the boulder away and came out only to find Sugrīva sitting on his throne. Angrily he banished Sugrīva into exile on Rushyamūka mountain and took his wife Tāra.

Mahishasura

Mahishasura was the buffalo-headed son of Diti. As Indra was destroying all her children, Diti went to the ashram of Supārswa and began performing tapas. Supārswa was annoyed at the utter intensity of Diti's tapas and cursed her that her son would be a buffalo. Brahma though was pleased with her tapas, and so blessed her with a powerful son who would have the head of a buffalo and the body of a human. Mahishasura grew up, made fierce tapas to Shiva, and told him that he did not want to die. Shiva refused to grant his request saying that all that is born must die. Mahishasura then asked that he should be killed by a woman and Shiva granted that request. There was no woman powerful enough to kill him. Mahishasura went to war with Indra, conquered him, and was enjoying the comforts of heaven. He was not kind to the Devas and was persecuting them. Knowing that he could only be killed by a woman, the Devas began praying for a female spirit and when that was formed, they called her Devi and gave her all of their weapons. Thus Devi riding a lion, fought Mahishasura and she killed him.

Mandōdari

Mandōdari was the daughter of Maya and Hema. Rāvana fell in love with Mandōdari and asked for her hand. They were married and had several sons, the eldest being Indrajit. Mandōdari was one of the great Pativratas. Rāvana was performing a great sacrifice and asked several rishis to donate blood. The blood was kept in a pot and Rāvana got another pot of milk blessed to beget a daughter from Kritsnamada. He mixed them and gave the pot to Mandōdari telling her it was poison and she should watch it carefully. Mandōdari felt belittled and drank that mixture of blood and milk. She became pregnant and did not wish to tell Rāvana so she went to her parents until the child was born. She put the child in a golden box and buried it. The box was later found by Janaka and the child was Sīta. Vāli fought with Rāvana and took Mandōdari as his wife and their son was Angada. During the great battle between Rāma and Rāvana, Rāvana was performing a special ritual to obtain powerful weapons. Just before completion of the ritual Angada, being a son of Mandōdari went to her and dragged her before Rāvana, because only a son or husband could touch a Pativrata. It made him so angry that he stopped the ritual and went to fight Rāma.

Manmadha

Manmadha was the son of Vishnu. Seeking a child, Vishnu prayed to Shiva and when Shiva granted him a child, Pārvati was angry because Vishnu did not pray to her. Pārvati cursed Manmadha that he would be killed by Shiva himself. When Vishnu objected and begged her to reverse, she did, but Manmadha would be invisible to all except his wife and parents. Manmadha's wife was Rati and his weapons were flowers. Manmadha is none other than Cupid. When Shiva was a guest of Himavantha, Pārvati was assigned to attend to his needs. Once when Shiva was meditating, Manmadha shot an arrow between Shiva and Pārvati. Shiva felt strange and looked at Manmadha, and in anger for disturbing his meditation he fused Manmadha with his third eye. When Rati (Manmadha's wife) begged Shiva she was granted to see Manmadha in full form. Otherwise, he would be invisible for all but kept on creating love feelings.

Maya

Maya was the son of Kasyapa and Diti. Though a Daitya, he was gentle and became a great sculptor and architect. He designed the great hall for the Pāndavas where Duryodhana was confused and took it as an insult. He created the beautiful city of Dwāraka for Krishna. Owing to his good deeds, the Devas gave him Hema; he built a castle for her and lived in it. They had two sons Māyavi and Dundubhi and a daughter Mandōdari. When Hema died, he went to the forest for meditation with his daughter. Rāvana saw

198

Mandōdari and fell in love with her. Maya had a brother Namuchi and they were living in Khāndava when Agni consumed it. Namuchi escaped but Maya could not.

Menaka

Menaka was one of the Apsaras serving Indra. She was sent often to disturb great rishis' rituals and tapas. She was sent to disturb Viswāmitra, which she did. Menaka and Viswāmitra had a daughter named Damayanti. Menaka left her child and went back to Indra's court.

Menaka (2)

Menaka was the granddaughter of Daksha. Once she and her two sisters were visiting Vishnu at the same time as the Sanatkumaras. The women did not show respect to the Sanatkumaras and were thus cursed to be born as humans. They begged for mercy, and were told that Menaka would become the wife of Himavanta and their daughter Pārvati would redeem Menaka.

Midhila

Midhila was a city ruled by Janaka.

Mitravinda

Mitravinda was one of Krishna's wives.

Mohini

When the ocean was churned and nectar came out of it, the Devas and the Danavas were quarreling to get to the nectar. Vishnu came as Mohini (also Jaganmohini -the enticing one) and asked them to sit in two rows. The Danavas were so mesmerized at Mohini's beauty that they almost forgot why they were there. In the meantime Mohini distributed the nectar to the Devas making them deathless. However two Danavas, Rāhu and Kētu slipped into the Devas line between the Sun and Moon and sipped the nectar. Knowing this, the Sun and Moon signaled with their eyes to Mohini that these were not Devas. Mohini chopped off their heads, but since they had already drunk the nectar, their heads remained alive. Since then, they regularly harass both the Sun and Moon through eclipses.

When Shiva heard of this feat by Vishnu, he prayed to Vishnu to show him how Mohini looked. Vishnu suddenly disappeared, and Shiva was searching for him and saw this great beauty instead. He fell in love with Mohini and began chasing her even to the point of ejaculation, out of which was born Kālabhairava. After understanding what had happened, Shiva prayed to Vishnu for forgiveness.

Mrukanda

Mrukanda was the son of Vidhāta and Niyati. He married Manaswini and after great tapas, they had a son Mārkandeya.

Mrutyuvu

The earth (Bhūmi) went to Brahma and begged him to reduce her burden. Brahma was puzzled and did not know how to do this. This made Bhūmi angry and out of him came a red colored woman. Brahma named her Mrutyuvu and asked her to kill people to reduce the burden of Bhūmi. When Mrutyuvu protested that women should give birth to people and not kill them, Brahma assured her that it was intended as a good deed. Mrutyuvu asked Brahma to create greed, anger, jealousy, envy, and disease through which she would do his bidding and destroy people.

Murāsura

Murāsura was also known as Bhasmāsura. He prayed to Brahma and received the power to annihilate whomever he touched. Once the power was granted, he tried to test it on Brahma himself. Brahma ran to Vishnu and Murāsura followed him. Vishnu saw them and asked Murāsura why he was so afraid because his heart was beating so loudly. Murāsura replied that he was not afraid and said "my heart is not beating loudly and touched it". He was immediately burnt to ashes.

Nārada

Nārada was a son of Brahma, born from his thigh. He had no family; he roamed the three worlds playing music and helping others. Nārada helped Dharmaja on several occasions. He was the one who prescribed how Draupadi should live with her five husbands. He was also the one who helped Rāma and Lakshmana when they were felled unconscious by Indrajit. Nārada helped many others in their times of grief and difficulty.

Nārada was also known to be an instigator of quarrels and a provocateur of fights among gods, demons, and kings. He reveled in spreading rumors. Once he went to Jalandhara and suggested that he should take Pārvati as his wife because Shiva did not deserve her. A fight ensued between Shiva and Jalandhara and the latter was killed. Nārada went to Rāvana and told him how all the Devas were torturing the Danavas, especially Yama and that he should fight Yama and save his kinsmen. A bit later, Nārada went to Yama and told him how Rāvana was preparing to fight him. He was the one who instigated the fight between Jarāsandha and Krishna.

Nārada was known for his musical talent which he got from Krishna. His great rival was Tumbura whom he could never exceed. He prayed to Vishnu and was told when Vishnu incarnates as Krishna, he would teach Nārada special lessons one of which was to make him an untalented musician.

Nārada realized that it was only to make him better by removing jealousy from him. Nārada once requested Vishnu to show him the illusion of life. He became a woman, married, and had children. He lost his children in fights and to disease, and felt very sad. Suddenly Vishnu appeared and made Nārada aware that the whole thing was an illusion. Nārada was among the great rishis and thus was a Maharshi.

Nārāyana

Nārāyana was another name for Vishnu. (see Nara)

Nahusha

Nahusha was a great Brahmin king who performed many sacrifices and achieved divinity. When Indra was dethroned, the Devas chose Nahusha as the replacement for Indra. He ruled the heavens well, but in time became complacent and even began insulting the great rishis. He fell in love with Sachi and asked her to marry him. She said she would marry him if he came to her in a palanquin carried by the great rishis. He ordered the rishis to carry him and when they refused, he kicked Agastya on the head. Agastya cursed him to become a serpent and he would become a man again when his questions were answered. He caught Bhīma and when even the strength of Bhīma could not free him, Dharnaja came and answered all his questions. Immediately the serpent became man and blessed both Bhīma and Dharmaja.

Nakula

Nakula was the son of Paandu and Mādri. He was actually Mādri's son by Aswinis. Nakula was an expert on horses and was taught the science of horses (Aswasāstra) by Sālihotra. His weakness was that he admired his own appearance too much.

Nala

Nala was the King of Nishadha and the son of Vīrasena. Once Nala caught a swan and the swan begged him to be let go. If Nala let the swan go, the swan would sing Nala's praises to Damayanti, one of the most beautiful princesses of that time. Damayanti was determined to marry Nala and when the marriage was advertised, even the Devas came to be selected by her and assumed the form of Nala. However, Damayanti begged the Devas to show her who the real Nala was, and when shown she married him. They lived happily until Kali, who was also an admirer of Damayanti found out and decided to hurt Nala. He arranged a poker game between Nala and his cousin Pushkara with the condition that whoever loses, he should go the forests for the rest of life. Nala was tricked and lost, so he went to the forests with his wife and two children. One day he was trying to catch a couple of birds and to do so he threw his clothes over them. They flew away with his clothes, so Damayanti cut her sari in half gave one half to Nala. He could not bear that his family was enduring such hardship, so one night he crept out and left them hoping Damayanti would go to her father and at least live in some comfort. Nala wandered away and soon

encounterd a snake, Karkotaka who was trapped by fire. Nala
rescued Karkotaka and when he did, the snake bit him and Nala
became ugly. The snake assured him that he would get his
beautiful form back when he needed it and that the ugly form was
for his own good. Nala assumed an alias Bahuka and entered the
court of Rutuparna as a cook. In the mean time Damayanti sent a
squad of Brahmins to find Nala. When they entered the city of
Rutuparna, they could see Bahuka and guessed correctly that he
was none other than Nala.

Now a plan was conceived to advertise a second marriage for
Damayanti and Rutuparna was invited. The distance was too
great for ordinary people, so Nala volunteered to drive
Rutuparna's chariot. On the way Nala learned numerology from
Rutuparna and taught him the science of horses. When they
finally reached Vidarbha, Damayanti secretly met Nala and
taunted him about what kind of man was he to leave his wife and
children in the forest and run away. Nala countered with what
kind of princess was she to declare marriage a second time when
the first husband was alive and still married to her. She then
declared the truth that it was a ploy to get him return to Vidarbha
and he was the only man she loved. At that point Nala asked
Karkotaka to give him his form back. Soon he challenged his
cousin to a poker game, and since he had learned numerology, he
won easily and recaptured his kingdom. Both Nala and Bhīma
became cooks and they were considered among the best chefs.

Namuchi

Namuchi was the son of Kasyapa and a friend of Bali. In the first battle between Bali and Indra, Namuchi nearly defeated Indra and made him unconscious, but then Indra killed Namuchi using his Vajra in the form of foam.

Nanda

Nanda was a shephard in Vrepalli and was married to Yasoda. Krishna was placed in Yasoda's bed by Vasudeva after his birth. Nanda and Yasoda raised Krishna as their own son. (see Krishna)

Nandi

Nandi was the bull on which Shiva rode. This bull also assumed the role of gatekeeper to Shiva and Pārvati. Nandi was found by Shilada while he was tilling a field. The boy grew up and prayed to Shiva intensely and when Shiva appeared and aksed for his wishes, the boy asked to be near Shiva from then on and be able to carry him. Nandi assumed the form of a bull to carry Shiva and to be his gatekeeper. This is why all Shiva temples have Nandi in the courtyard.

Nandini

Nandini was the daughter (cow) of Kāmadhenu in Vasishta's ashram. Whoever drank its milk would become immortal. When king Dilipa wanted to have children, he served Nandini. (see Dilipa)

Nara and Nārāyana

Both Nara and Nārāyana were from Vishnu's body. After the incarnation of half-lion, half-man to destroy Hiranyakasipa, Vishnu's body fell apart. The human part became Nara and the lion's part became Nārāyana. They were friends and almost inseparable. While they were performing tapas, Indra tried to discourage them and so sent a squad of apsaras to seduce them. Nara and Nārāyana knew Indra's trick, so Nārāyana scratched his thigh and out came the most beautiful woman, more beautiful than the apsaras. She was Urvasi. The apsaras were ashamed and went away. There was a rākshasa called Sahasrakavacha (thousand armored one). In order to penetrate each of the armors, one had to complete a thousand years of tapas. Nara and Nārāyana took turns each for one thousand years at a time and penetrated all but one armor. The rākshasa was born as Karna with natural armor and Nara and Nārāyana came as Krishna and Arjuna to kill Karna. (see Karna)

Narasimha

Narasimha was the fourth incarnation of Vishnu as half-man half-lion to kill Hiranyakasipa. (see Hiranyakasipa)

Nīla

Nīla was a monkey general who fought alongside Rāma. When the bridge Setu was being built, all the monkeys including Hanumān were bringing stones. Whatever Hanumān brought Nīla accepted with one hand. This angered Hanumān and so the next time he brought all the stones he could carry with his enormous strength. Even then Nīla took it all with one hand. Rāma saw the rivalry and diffused it by requesting Nīla to agree to use both hands. (see Hanumān)

Nimi

Nimi was a king of the Sun dynasty and the son of Ikshwaaka. He intended to perform a yagna, and asked Vasishta to be the head priest. Vasishta said he had another engagement, but would come soon after that. Meanwhile, Nimi approached Gautama and asked him to be the chief priest. During the ceremony Vasishta came, became angry with Nimi, and cursed him to be bodyless. Gautama preserved what was left of Nimi and completed the yagna. The Devas appeared and offered to revive Nimi but he refused saying that the body nurtures only ego, jealousy, and anger and he would not want any of them. He would appear to others as having a body and so he ruled his kingdom called Videha meaning bodyless one. His son was Janaka.

Oghāvati

Oghāvati was the daughter of Oghavanta and married her grandfather (father's father) Sudarshana. Sudarshana was intent on conquering death and asked Oghāvati to serve any guest who appeared at their door and please him any way he desired. To test the resolve of Sudarshana, Yama (god of death) came as a Brahmin and Oghāvati served him food, rubbed his feet, and gave him a massage. The guest was still not pleased because he wanted her to make love to him. Oghāvati was in a great dilemma to weigh her husband's orders against adultery. She asked the guest to come to a secret place where Sudarshana could see them without himself being seen. When they arrived, Sudarshana called out for Oghāvati and saw them together. At that point Yama assumed his own form and pronounced Sudarshana as conqueror of death. Oghāvati did not have any children.

Padma

Padma was the daughter of Anaranya. While wandering in the forest, she met a hermit Pippālada and he fell in love with her and asked her who she belonged to. When told, he went to Anaranya and asked him for her hand. Anaranya at first hesitated, but then gave her in marriage to Pippālada. Padma followed him to his ashram and one day Dharma wanted to test her. He appeared as a handsome prince and asked her to marry him and not waste her life with an old man. As she was a pativrata, Padma not only refused him but also taught him some moral lessons. At that point Dharma became himself and asked her what her wishes were. All she asked for was to please her husband and be happy.

Padmakalpa

Padmakalpa was the period of time when Brahma came out of Vishnu on a lotus flower and created the universe. Other periods were Brhmakalpa and Varāhakalpa.

Padmāvati

Padmāvati was the mother of Ambarīsha. She prayed to Vishnu to have a son who would be dedicated to him. That son was Ambarīsha.

Pāndu

Pāndu was the son of Ambālika and the father of the Pāndavas. When Vichitravīrya died without children, his mother Satyavati requested her other son Vyasa to produce sons with Ambika and Ambālika. Ambika's son was the blind king Dhrutarāshtra and Ambālika's was Pāndu (the pale one). Pāndu married Kunti and Mādri and was fond of hunting. On one such hunting trip, he saw two deer in the act of love and shot one of them. The other

210

became a human and told Pāndu that he had committed a bad deed by killing an animal while they were copulating and he should repent for it. Instead Pāndu argued and angered the human who happened to be a rishi called Kindama. Kindama cursed Pāndu that would die when he made love and his wife would die with him. He could not make love to his wives and as days went by, Kunti told him of her special gift to call any god and have a child from him. Pāndu agreed with her and she called first Yama, then Indra, and then Vāyu and had Dharmaja, Arjuna, and Bhīma. She also let Mādri have this benefit and she called for the Aswinis and thus Mādri had Nakula and Sahadeva. One day the beautiful Mādri was swimming naked and Pāndu could not resist the urge to make love to her. When he did, they both died instantly and Kunti raised all five children of Pāndu, who are called the Pāndavas. (see Kunti)

Pārvati

Pārvati was the wife of Shiva and daughter of Himavanta. In her previous life she was Sati, the eldest daughter of Daksha and also the wife of Shiva. When Daksha humiliated Sati for showing up uninvited, Sati became embarrassed, angry, and committed self-immolation. All of the Devas were concerned that Shiva was alone and they all went to Brahma and asked him for help. Brahma assured them that Sati would be born as Pārvati to

Himavanta and Menaka. When Pārvati became of age, Himavanta asked Shiva to come and spend some time in meditation at his place and he also ordered Pārvati to serve him. As this was going on, Manmadha (cupid) shot an arrow at Shiva and Pārvati. Shiva felt the distraction, saw its origin, and immediately destroyed Manmadha with his third eye. All of the Devas and even Brahma begged Shiva to reconsider his feelings towards Pārvati and soon after that they were married. Shiva stayed with Himavanta for some time until he established his own place at Kailas.

Once Pārvati was taking a ceremonial bath and she made a small statue with starch and brought it to life. She installed that statue at the gate with strict orders not to let any one in. When Shiva returned and wanted to get in, the little boy would not allow him. Shiva cut his head off and went inside. He then casually asked who the boy at the gate was. Pārvati replied "he is our boy, I must ask him to come in". Shiva told her it was too late and to please her he sent his armies to find any creature that was sleeping with its head facing North. They went out and brought back an elephant head, which Shiva fixed to the torso of the boy. This was Ganesha, the elephant-headed god. Pārvati adopted him like her own son, which he was. (see Ganesha)

Once when Pārvati and Shiva were seriously in the mood to make love, Agni appeared and spoiled the act. An angry Pārvati threw the sperm mixture at Agni and asked him to bear the son. Agni could not and hid the fetus in the sawgrass. Their other son, Kumāraswāmi was born out of the sawgrass. (see Agni and Kumāraswāmi)

Parāsara

Parāsara was the grandson of Vasishta. His mother never wore jewelry or ornaments. When Parāsara asked his mother about this, she told him that his father was killed by a rākshasa. Parāsara asked permission of his grandfather and set out to see his father. He prayed to Shiva and when Shiva appeared Parāsara asked for his wish to see his father. Shiva let him see for only a moment, then he decided to perform a great sacrifice to annihilate all the rākshasas. As their families were disappearing, all the rākshasas under the leadership of Pulastya came and begged him to stop the carnage.

One day on one of his pilgrimages, Parāsara had to cross the river Yamuna and there he saw a ferry maiden Satyavati and fell in love with her. She was not very clean and smelled of fish. Parāsara cleansed her with his powers and made love to her. A son was born immediately and that was Vyasa, the man who wrote all the Purānas and was a great vedic scholar. He bowed to his mother and promised her to appear any time she wished to see him and do her bidding, and then disappeared. It was this ability that Satyavati used to order Ambika and Ambālika to mate with Vyasa and produce Dhrutarāshtra and Pāndu. (see Satyavati)

Parasurāma

Parasurāma was the son of Jamadagni and Renuka. He was one of the incarnations of Vishnu and also the guru of martial arts. All of the famous warriors of Mahābhārata were his pupils. He had four brothers. Once Jamadagni suspected his wife of adultery and so ordered his sons to kill her. All four brothers refused, but Rāma went to his mother and cut her head off. A pleased Jamadgni asked Rāma for his wishes, and immediately Rāma asked for his mother to be alive again and his brothers to be excused for disobeying their father. After that he visited his grandfather Ruchika and great grandfather Bhrugu. They saw this brilliant boy and advised him to go to the Himalayas and pray to Shiva. As he was praying intensely, Shiva came as an old man to test him and disturbed him with loud noises and useless laughter to belittle him. Rāma was not distracted, instead he asked the old man to leave or sit with him and pray to Shiva. Arguments followed and Rāma recognized that the old man was none other than Shiva himself, so he prostrated himself before him. A pleased Shiva gave him special weapons and also taught him the martial arts. One of those weapons was parasu (the ax) and since then Rāma was known as Parasurāma.

Once when Rāma went into the forest, he had a premonition that something bad was going to happen. Upon his return, he saw his mother crying on the slain body of his father and beating her chest twenty-one times. Rāma swore that he would raid all of the kings twenty-one times and eradicate them, because it was the King Kārtavīrya who had killed his father. He was about to perform the funeral rights for his father, when Bhrugu himself appeared and revived Jamadagni and asked Rāma not to carry out his promise. Neverthless, Rāma went ahead and finished most of the kings including Kārtavīrya. He spared only the kings who were in marriage or in their nuptials. In order to avoid Parasurāma's attack, Dasaradha married a new bride everyday for 365 days until the attacks were over.

Rāma went to Agastya and there prayed to Vishnu who appeared and gave him Parasurāma's powers. Thus Parasurāma became an incarnation. These powers were to be taken away later when Parasurāma confronted Rāma.

After terminating most of the kings, Parasurāma went to the Narmada River to bathe in it to cleanse himself of the sin of killing kings. After bathing and performing mass funeral rites for the kings, he went to Kailas to visit Shiva and Pārvati. At the gate he met Ganesha who said to him it was not a good time to see his parents. Parasurāma became angry and a fight broke out between Ganesha and Parasurāma. Ganesha rolled his trunk around Parasurāma and lifted him high into the sky and started twirling to throw him. At this point Parasurāma took his ax and hit hard on Ganesha's tusks, and as a result one of the tusks fell down with a fierce thud. On hearing this, Shiva and Pārvati came out to see what had happened. They immediately pacified both Ganesha and Parasurāma, since then Ganesha had only one tusk (Ekadanta).

Dasaradha was returning to Ayodhya after the wedding of Rāma and Sīta. On the way Parasurāma appeared and demanded to finish Rāma. Dasaradha begged him for mercy but Parasurāma had none. He said to Rāma, "until now whenever that word Rāma was mentioned, it belonged to me. Now that there is another Rāma, I am ashamed at hearing that word. So shall I put you away?" and challenged Rāma to raise his bow. Rāma took it and spanned it without effort. In that transfer, all the strength of

Parasurāma entered into the other Rāma and Parasurāma went to the Himalayas to meditate and pray.

As he was traveling, Parasurāma was approached by Amba who asked him to help her marry Bhīshma. Parasurāma promised his help and asked Bhīshma, who was also his pupil to take Amba as his wife. Bhīshma refused saying that he took an oath never to marry. A fight ensued that lasted for twenty-four days and ended in a draw after the Devas and Brahma persuaded them to stop. (see Bhīshma and Amba)

Parīkshit

Parīkshit was the son of Abhimanya and Uttara. Abhimanya was killed before Parīkshit was born and Parīkshit was then protected by Krishna from Aswatthāma's revenge. He inherited the throne from Dharmaja and ruled for many years. One day while hunting he came across the hermit Shameeka who in his meditation did not pay any attention to people passing by. Parīkshit thought Shameeka was snubbing him so he picked up a dead snake and wrapped it around Shameeka's neck. Srungi, one of Shameeka's sons came and saw the dead snake, took it and threw it away. As Srungi did not know whom it was that had done this, he cursed the doer to die within a week by the bite of Takshaka, one of the most venomous snakes. When Shameeka heard this he immediately sent word to Parīkshit and warned him to take proper measures. Parīkshit made his castle impenetrable to snakes. He waited and listened to puraanas and Vedas. Takshaka entered the castle as a false Brahmin and offered a lemon fruit to Parīkshit and out of the fruit came a snake and bit him. (see

Kausika) After Parīkshit, his son Janamējaya became king.

Parvata

Parvata was the nephew of Nārada and also his good friend. During one of their travels, they saw Ambarīsha's daughter Srīmati and fell in love with her. Ambarīsha made it clear that only one of them could have her. They each secretly went to Vishnu and requested him to make the other one's face appear like that of a monkey. Vishnu obliged and when all of them appeared before Srīmati, she ignored the monkey faces and married Vishnu. When they found out, both Nārada and Parvata became angry and cursed Vishnu that he would lose his wife and find her only with the help of monkeys. (see Rāmāyana)

Parvata (2)

The Himalayan mountains and all high mountains were called parvatas. The daughter Himavatparvata is Pārvati.

Pasupati

Pasupati is another name for Shiva. It means lord of animals.

Pināka

Pināka was the name for Shiva's bow. When Kanva was meditating intensely, an anthill grew on him and out of that grew a bamboo plant. Brahma appeared before Kanva, blessed him, and made three bows out of that bamboo. He gave one to Shiva, one to Vishnu, and kept one for himself.

Prabhāvati

Prabhāvati was the daughter of Bharadwāja who insisted on marrying only Indra. Indra came as a young man and asked her to marry him. She refused by saying she would marry only Indra and he should go away. Indra wanted to test her, so he gave her some raw fruit and asked her to ripen it by fire. While she was doing that the firewood was burned out, but the fruit did not ripen. Afraid that the fire would be extinguished if she went away searching for wood, she kept the fire going by putting her feet in it. At that point Indra assumed his own form and took her to the heavens.

Pradyumna

Pradyumna was the son of Krishna and Rukmini. In a previous life he was Manmadha, son of Vishnu.

Prahlāda

Prahlāda was the son of Hiranyakasipa and Līlāvati. (see Hiranyakasipa) While Hiranyakasipa was praying to Brahma, Indra captured his empire and was about to kill Līlāvati who was pregnant with Prahlāda. The great Nārada intervened and told Indra not to do this because the child inside Līlāvati was going to be one of the greatest disciples of Vishnu. Hiranyakasipa regained his kingdom, defeated Indra and several others, and was ruling all three worlds ruthlessly. He engaged the great guru Chandāmarka to teach Prahlāda, and under his tutelage Prahlāda became a scholar in many subjects and also a firm Vishnu disciple. There was no way to dissuade Prahlāda from chanting praises to Vishnu. Hiranyakasipa did not like this and in order to teach Prahlāda a lesson he tortured his own son and forbade him from ever uttering the name Vishnu again. Prahlāda was not to be intimidated by such things and kept singing the praises of Vishnu. Fed up with his behavior, one day at dusk Hiranyakasipa asked Prahlāda to show him the Vishnu he prays to so often so that he could settle the matter once and for all. Prahlāda replied that the god Vishnu is wherever one seeks to find him. At that point a furious Hiranyakasipa retaliated "is this Vishnu of yours in this pillar which is one of the many in the castle?" Prahlāda replied "yes sir he is there and everywhere". Hiranyakasipa in a rage pulled his sword and slashed the pillar. Out came Narasimha who was half-human and half-lion. He grabbed Hiranyakasipa, laid him on his lap and tore him with his claws. During that fierce fight Hiranyakasipa protested that Narasimha had twenty claws whereas he had only two hands. Vishnu replied that in the next life he would have twenty hands and shall be killed by a common king with two hands. Hiranyakasipa came as Rāvana with ten heads and twenty hands, while Vishnu came as Rāma with two hands. (see Rāvana)

On one of his pilgrimages, Prahlāda saw the weapons in front of Nara and Nārāyana. He immediately thought these were not sages because sages do not need weapons. Prahlāda argued with them and was about to fight with them when Vishnu appeared and told him the truth that both Nara and Nārāyana were parts of Narasimha and they had their mission to carry weapons to destroy Sahasrakavacha. (see Karna)

Prahlāda's grandson was Bali who was also destroyed by Vishnu as the dwarf Brahmin Vāmana.

Pulaha

Pulaha was the son of Brahma born from his navel. He married Gati, daughter of Kardama and their children were Kinnaras and Kimpurushas.

Pulastya

Pulastya was the son of Brahma and born from his ears. Once when he was meditating at the ashram of Trunabindu, many a maiden came singing and dancing to disturb him. He angrily cursed them that whoever appeared in his sight, their virginity would be destroyed. They were afraid and left him. However the daughter of Trunabindu was passing by without any knowledge of the curse and Pulastya saw her. She became pregnant immediately and was ashamed to face her father. Trunabindu learned the truth and offered her to Pulastya in marriage. Their son was Visrāvasu and his son was Rāvana.

Pushpadanta

Pushpadanta was the king of Yugandhara and an ardent disciple of Shiva. He became the king of burial grounds and funerals because of a mistake. (see Bhetāla)

Pūru

Pūru was the youngest son of Yayāti and Sharmishta. When Yayāti's other wife Devayāni found out that Yayāti was spending more time with Sharmishta and not her, she angrily went to her father Sukra and told him how humiliated she was. Sukra cursed Yayāti to become an old man immediately. He would be able to borrow anyone's youth and enjoy sensual pleasures. Yayāti begged his other sons who turned him down, but Pūru without any hesitation gave his youth to Yayāti. Yayāti enjoyed the bodily pleasures for a long time and then Pūru was installed as king. Pūru was one of the four great givers, the others were Bali, Karna, and Sibi.

Pūtana

Pūtana was a rākshasa woman and a friend of Kamsa. When Kamsa knew that a child was growing in Vrepalli who would kill him, he sent many rākshasas to find out more about the child and to kill the child. Pūtana was one such demon. She assumed the shape of a human and went to Vrepalli. There she inquired about all the children as if she was very fond of them and was even nursing some. Whomever she nursed, they died instantly. When it was Krishna's turn, the little boy sucked all of her strength until she fell dead showing her real form.

Rādha

Rādha was Krishna's lover. In a previous life she was Sachi who expressed the desire to sit on Vishnu's lap. She came as Rādha who was also Krishna's aunt. The great love affair of Rādha and Krishna was the subject of many stories and paintings. As the story goes Krishna was only eight years old when Rādha (at eighteen plus) seduced him and presumably she taught him the art of love making.

Rāhu

Rāhu was one of the rākshasas who slipped into the line of devas along with his friend Ketu to drink nectar served them by Vishnu as Jaganmohini *(his female avatar, the world's most beautiful woman).* The fact that these two were not devas was signaled by the Sun and Moon (Chandra) to Vishnu. Immediately Vishnu cut them down with his Chakra, but it was too late as they had already drunk the nectar. Their heads were immortal and Brahma awarded them the status of a planet. Since it was the Sun and Moon who betrayed them, they regularly tortured the Sun and Moon by eclipsing them. (see Ketu)

Rāma

Rāma was the son of Dasaradha and Kausalya and the seventh incarnation of Vishnu. Rāma had three half-brothers: Bharata son of Kaikeyi, and Lakshmana and Satrughna, sons of Sumitra. They all grew up as brothers and loved each other very much. One day Viswāmitra came to Dasaradha and asked that Rāma and Lakshmana be sent with him to protect his yagnya. Rāma was only fourteen and so Dasaradha was hesitant, but Viswāmitra assured him that they would be safe. Viswāmitra taught them archery and the use of special weapons. When the ritual began, the Rākshasi Tātaka came by to disturb the rites, but was driven away by Rāma. After the successful completion of the yagnya, Viswāmitra took them to the city of Mithila which was ruled by King Janaka. King Janaka had just proclaimed that whoever could bend the big bow he had set up would be allowed to marry his beautiful daughter Sīta. Many princes and even some kings tried but were unable to even lift the bow. Urged by Viswāmitra, Rāma went up to the bow, lifted it, and bent it until it broke. Janaka was very pleased that it was Rāma who won the contest because he was a handsome young man and very suitable in every way to marry Sīta. An elaborate ceremony was arranged and Dasaradha came with a huge entourage for the wedding because three royal princesses were found for the brothers of Rāma. After the ceremonies and nuptials, Dasaradha returned to Ayodhya with his newly acquired daughters-in-law. On the way a brilliant light suddenly shone and Parasurāma appeared before them. Angrily he challenged Rāma to take his bow and try to span it. As he was passing the bow, his brilliance and powers also passed to Rāma.

Shortly after returning to Ayodhya, Dasaradha wanted to crown Rāma as king and abdicate the throne. Dates were set for the ceremonies and everyone was happy including Kaikeyi. Kaikeyi's maid Mandhara came into her chambers and gave her some bad advice. She asked Kaikeyi what would be the fate of her own son Bharata as an unimportant member of the royal family and what would her own status be? Mandhara advised Kaikeyi that she should demand Dasaradha honor the promises he made her a long time ago. She should insist on sending Rāma to the forests for fourteen years and make her son Bharata the king. When Dasaradha heard these demands, he was crestfallen but kept his promise and told Rāma what must happen. Rāma said he would never disobey his father's orders and got himself ready to go to

226

the forests.   Needless to say Sīta and Lakshmana joined him. Their departure devastated Dasaradha, who died screaming for his son because he was also cursed to die in that manner. (see Dasaradha)

All that time Bharata was not in Ayodhya, he was visiting with his uncle to enjoy mangoes and other summer fruits. He was summoned back to Ayodhya immediately and when he arrived he found out what had happened. His father was dead, his brother Rāma was sent to the forests, and his mothers were in mourning. He was a very wise man and also loved Rāma very much. He was heartbroken at the events and set out to bring Rāma back and crown him as king. He went with his entourage to fetch Rāma. As they were trying to cross the river Ganga, the ferryman Guha did not want to ferry them at first. He thought Bharata was going to fight with Rāma, but when told the truth he did ferry them. (see Guha) Bharata begged Rāma to come back and rule the kingdom, but Rāma said it was their father's order and he would not disobey it. Bharata asked Rāma to give him his sandals which he placed on the throne and ruled in the name of Rāma for fourteen years and not a day more.

Rāma did the funeral rites for his father and then started to move as it would lessen his sorrow. On their way they visited Vasishta, his wife Arundhati gave some secrets to Sīta on how to serve her husband and also gave her a special flower which would always keep her fresh. After leaving Vasishta's ashram Rāma, Sīta, and Lakshmana entered the Dandaka forest and built a small ashram there. They were quite happy thinking, meditating, and practicing archery. One day Sūrpanaka, sister of Rāvana came by and she

227

fell in love with Rāma. She begged him to take her as a second wife or even as a mistress. Rāma refused her and suggested she should talk to Lakshmana, which she did only to be insulted and defaced by him. Hurt and angry she went to Lanka and told her brother what had happened and also how beautiful Sīta was and that he should get her as his queen. Rāvana thought of a trick and asked his uncle and Tataka's son Māricha to play a deer and wander near their ashram. Sīta saw the deer and felt like having it. She mentioned that to Rāma, who immediately went chasing the deer. Soon they heard a shriek. Sīta fearing the worst, asked Lakshmana to go and see what had happened. Lakshmana said to her that it was all some kind of trick and she should not worry because Rāma was safe. At that point Sīta became angry and ordered Lakshmana to go and see. Soon after that Rāvana came disguised as a Brahmin and asked for some rice. While Sīta was giving him the rice, he snatched her, put her on his chariot parked out of sight, and began driving to Lanka. Sīta was crying loudly that she was Dasaradha's daughter-in-law and a strange man was kidnapping her. She bundled up all of her jewelry and dropped it as a sign to Rāma and Lakshmana. Her cries were heard by Jatāyuvu the great vulture, who immediately came to her rescue and began tearing Rāvana apart. Rāvana was more powerful and with a mighty stroke of his sword he cut Jatāyuvu down.

Rāma and Lakshmana returned to their ashram and found Sīta missing. They called her name loudly, but there was no sign of her. They began walking along the tracks of the chariot. On their way they encountered a strange creature that was only a big belly and two long arms that could reach any length. This was Kabandha who when they cut his arms off, he assumed his original form. He blessed them and advised them to go to

228

Rushyamūka and make friends with the monkey king Sugrīva. (see Kabandha) A few days later, they met Jatāyuvu who was near death. He told them that Rāvana had kidnapped Sīta and driven away to Lanka, and then he breathed his last. Rāma performed the last rites for Jatāyuvu and set out to Rushyamūka.

As they were nearing Rushyamūka, a very large monkey greeted them and introduced himself as Hanumantha and said he would take them to Sugrīva, which he did. Sugrīva greeted them with respect, and told of his problem. His problem was that he was at loggerheads with his brother Vāli who stole his wife. He would like to conquer Vāli and regain his wife and the kingdom of Kishkindha. Lakshmana said that Rāma could help him, but Sugrīva told them it was not an easy matter to fight Vāli. Whoever fights with him face-to-face would loose half of his strength to Vāli. Vāli could easily defeat anyone. At that Rāma assured Sugrīva that he would be invisible to Vāli and shoot him from behind. Sugrīva challenged his brother Vāli to a fight and as the fight went on, Vāli was winning and Sugrīva was getting weaker and weaker. Finally he ran away and confronted Rāma, asking him what he was doing. Rāma then said that both Vāli and Sugrīva looked alike and he could not distinguish one from the other. The next time they fought, Sugrīva wore a garland around his neck. This time it was easy for Rāma, who was hiding behind a tree when Vāli was fighting, to shoot Vali in the back. A fallen Vāli looked at Rāma and asked why he shot him. He said "I never knew you or even your problem. If it is only getting Sīta from Rāvana, I would whip him and get her in no time. Why do you have to kill me?" For that Rāma did not have a good answer, but then Vāli requested Rāma that he had a son Angada and he should take care of him. Rāma promised that and Vāli died soon after.

229

As promised, Sugrīva sent his armies in all directions in order to discover the whereabouts of Sīta. They searched far and wide and finally came to the ocean. There they saw an old vulture who wanted to feast on a few monkeys. When told of their purpose, the vulture who was Sampāti, brother of Jatāyuvu told them that Rāvana had taken her across the ocean to Lanka. They had to figure out how to cross the ocean and find Sīta. This task went to Hanuman, who jumped the ocean into Lanka and was searching for Sīta. He saw her under an ashoka tree (member of the family of tulip trees) guarded by a Rakshasa women. He also saw Rāvana come by and ask her to marry him. She was crying and chanting Rāma, Rāma. Hanuman approached her slowly and told her he was Rāma's messenger. At first she did not believe him, but then he showed her Rāma's ring. He offered to carry her on his back right away, but she did not like that idea. She gave him one jewel she kept with her as proof that she was still alive and waiting for Rāma to come. By that time the news of Hanuman in Lanka spread and he was caught and brought forth before Rāvana. Rāvana admonished him and lit his tail on fire, because he would not kill a messenger. This gave Hanuman the idea of jumping from one building to another and sitting on them until they caught fire. Thus he nearly destroyed Lanka before flying back.

Soon Rāma assembled an army of monkeys and bears with the help of Sugrīva and Jāmbavanta and arrived at the shores of the ocean. He had to build a bridge and he did so by dropping stones. (see Hanumanta and Nīla) There was a small squirrel always rolling in the sand and dipping in the water. Rāma saw this,

230

caught the squirrel and asked what it was doing. The squirrel replied "I am trying to help you. I am not as big as those monkeys, but I can always hold a bit of sand and put it in the water." A touched Rāma thanked and stroked the squirrel with his three fingers. (Some believe that is why squirrels have three stripes) Rāma crossed the bridge and sent another messenger to Rāvana that he should return Sīta and avoid all bloodshed. Rāvana had a brother called Vibhīshana who advised him to do as Rāma asked. Rāvana ignored all of these suggestions, banished Vibhīshana, and prepared for the war.

It was brutal, several monkeys and rakshasas died. Rāvana's son Indrajit fought ferociously killing many of the monkey leaders until finally Lakshmana killed him. Another brother Kumbhakarna was also tricked into death. Rāma had no special weapons, so Agastya showed him the worship of the Sun so Rāma could get a chariot and special weapons. Meanwhile Rāvana was performing a Yagnya to get the indestructible golden chariot. Knowing that if he succeeded there was no way to kill him, Angaga went to the queens chambers and dragged Mandōdari before Rāvana. (see Angada and Mandōdari)

Rāvana was furious because he could not bear insulting his wife. He broke off the yagnya and went directly to battle with Rāma. His power was so great, that at one time he felled both Rāma and Lakshmana unconscious. Nīla revived them with special medicine Sanjivi brought by Hanumān. Next day Rāma was fierce and was cutting off the heads of Rāvana (he had ten heads and also called Dasakantha meaning ten-headed), but they were cropping up again and again. Rāma was puzzled, he did not know what to do.

At that point, Vibhīshana told Rāma that he should aim at Rāvana's stomach first, because Rāvana stole the nectar and hid it in his stomach. Thus he could not be killed unless the nectar was destroyed first. After that, it was matter of minutes, Rāvana was killed by Rāma. There were three great sinners; Parasurāma who killed his mother, Prahlāda who aided killing his father, and Vibhīshana who betrayed his brother.

Soon after the war, Rāma took Sītā and went back to Ayodhya in the Pushpaka Vimāna, Rāvana's flying chariot. He just barely made it before Bharata was about to jump into the fire as Rāma was a bit late. Rāma was crowned and assumed the rule of Ayodhya. His reign was known as the best reign and hence any best rule is called Rāma Raj. Rāma ruled quite long and the devas in heavens wanted him back. So they created a gossip about Sītā and forced Rāma to abandon Sītā even though she was pregnant. Lakshmana drove Sītā to the ashram of Vasishta and she gave birth to twins Lava and Kusha. When Rāma was performing a horse yagnya, the great Vālmīki brought the two boys and Rāma felt an immediate affection to them. When asked Vālmīki told him the truth and also brought Sītā before Rāma. Rāma was confused, and even before he could compose and think, Sītā bowed to his feet and prayed to her mother Earth to take her away. It was unbelievable; the Earth split open and Sītā vanished into that fault. A saddened Rāma took his children and was planning to crown them. Then one day Yama came and asked for a very private audience with Rāma while Lakshmana watched the door. Any way he was disturbed and Lakshmana was sent into exile and drowned in the river Sarayu. (see Lakshmana) Soon Rāma abdicated the throne in favor of his sons and set out to go into the forest. But while crossing the river Sarayu, there was a quick flood and Rāma along with his entourage of Bharata, Satrughna, and many others drowned.

Rāmāyana

Rāmāyana was the story of Rāma as written by Vālmīki. This was also the first verse written in Sanskrit by the first poet (Adi Kavi).

Rāvana

Rāvana was the Rākshasa king of Lanka. He was the grandson of Pulastya and also half-brother of Kubera. Rāvana was born with ten heads and twenty arms and so was named Dasakantha and he had two brothers Kumbhakarna and Vibhīshana, and a sister Sūrpanaka. Rāvana was Hiranyakasipa in his previous life. When Vishnu came as Narasimha (lion-man) to kill Hiranyakasipa, he protested to Vishnu that he came with twenty claws and sneaked from behind to kill him. Vishnu said that in the next life he would come with twenty arms and ten heads, and Vishnu would come as an ordinary man to kill him. Thus Rāvana had ten heads. Rāvana was an ardent Brahmin practicing all of the rituals. He set out to perform the greatest tapas for Brahma. He was sacrificing one of his heads everytime and finally had only one head left. The world was trembling when Rāvana was about to sacrifice his last head. Suddenly Brahma appeared and asked for his wishes. He wished that he would not be killed by the Devas or Yakshas or Gandharvas (all heavenly types), for he never suspected that he would be killed by a human.

With all of his newly acquired strength, he met some rakshasas who told him of the city Kubera built in Lanka and they urged him to drive off Kubera and occupy Lanka. He sent word to Kubera expressing his wishes and Kubera gladly left, blessing him. Shortly after however, Kubera sent a message to Rāvana that his reign was cruel and people were suffering. At that point Rāvana fought Kubera, defeated him, and stole his flying chariot, Pushpaka. Rāvana was riding his newly acquired plane and went to Kailas, Shiva's residence. There he saw Nandi who told him that Shiva was dancing and should not be disturbed. Rāvana laughed loudly and then took Kailas in his hands and began shaking it. At that point, Shiva became annoyed and pressed the mountain with his toe. This crushed Rāvana's hands and he cried so loudly that the world shook. He then prayed to Shiva and received his blessings.

Rāvana was power drunk and began fighting with many kings and emperors. One day he met Nārada who told him of the impending birth of Vishnu to Kausalya. Rāvana kidnapped Kausalya and put her in a box that was found by Dasaradha. Dasaradha later married Kausalya. They were rescued from a flood by Jatāyuvu. He then went on to fight with Indra who defeated him and tied him up. His son Meghanādha came and fought with Indra and rescued his father. Meghanādha has since been known as Indrajit. Soon after this Rāvana sent Vāli a message to recognize him as the unconquerable. Vāli replied "try me" and needless to say Vāli picked up Rāvana and drowned him in the seven seas. A shaken Rāvana begged for mercy and became a friend of Vāli. Vāli later took Rāvana's wife Mandōdari.

Raghu

Raghu was the son of Dilīpa and great-grandfather of Rāma. He conquered both Kubera and Indra to help his father's yagnya. Because of his greatness, the dynasty of Rāma was called Raghu dynasty.

Rambha

Rambha was the most beautiful apsara. She was sent by Indra to distract others from their tapas.

Rati

Rati was the wife of Manmadha. When Manmadha was scorched by Shiva, Rati begged him to restore her husband. Shiva granted her wish, but only she could see Manmadha as he used to be. This is why cupid has no form.

Reibhya

Reibhya was the son of Sumati and the father of Dushyanta.

Reivata

Reivata was the son of Anarta and had a daughter named Revati. He designed a beautiful city in the middle of the ocean. Reivata was having difficulty deciding who should marry his daughter Revati, so he took her to Brahma and was asked to wait a moment to see him. When he told Brahma about his mission, Brahma said in that moment on the earth all four yugas went by in three cycles and all the eligible bachelors on earth had passed away. There was one decendent of Nārāyana and he should give Revati in marriage to him. His name was Balabhadra and they had several children.

Renuka

Renuka was the wife of Jamadagni and the mother of their five children: Ramanvata, Sushena, Vasu, Viswavasu, and Rāma. One day Renuka was fetching water from the river and came upon prince Chitraradha who was bathing. He was a handsome prince so she was looking at him longingly and hence became very late in fetching the water to Jamadagni. In a jealous rage Jamadagni ordered his sons to kill their mother by cutting off her head. One

237

by one each of the four sons refused and in turn was cursed by Jamadagni. When it was Rāma's turn, he cut off Renuka's head without hesitation and presented it to his father. Jamadagni was so pleased, he asked Rāma for two wishes. Rāma immediately asked to restore his mother's life and remove the curses on his brothers.

Rohini

Rohini was the wife of Vasudeva and mother of Krishna and Balaraama. In a previous life she was Kadruva.

Rohita

Rohita was the son of Harischandra and Chandramati. He was born as a gift of Varuna and was to be sacrificed in a ritual. Harischandra continued to delay the ritual and when Rohita discovered this, he prayed for Indra to relieve his father from the obligation to Varuna. (see Harischandra) He was also known as Lōhitaasya.

Rudra

Rudra was another name for Shiva and there were eleven different Rudras. They were Aja, Ekapaada, Ahirbudhya, Tvashtra, Rudra, Sambhu, Hara, Tryambaka, Aparājita, Eshana, and Tribhuva.

Rukmi

Rukmi was the brother of Rukmini and a friend of Sisupāla. Her brother wanted her to marry Sisupāla but she was in love with Krishna. She sent a message to Krishna that time was running out unless he somehow appeared and took her away. Krishna came and kidnapped Rukmini. At that point Rukmi was angry and fought with Krishna and lost. Instead of killing him Krishna shaved his head and sent him away. For revenge Rukmi tried to fight with Krishna by offering his services to Duryodhana and was refused. Finally Rukmi sought a gambling session with Balarāma and lost, but picked a fight in which he was slain by Balarāma.

Rukmini

Rukmini was the sister of Rukmi and the principal wife of Krishna. (see Krishna)

Sālva

Sālva was the son of Damaghosha and brother of Sisupāla. He fell in love with Amba and when Amba returned from Bhīshma after her kidnapping, Sālva refused to marry her. (see Amba) After his brother Sisupāla was killed by Krishna, Sālva performed great tapas and obtained several boons from Shiva. Armed with that strength, Sālva went to Dwaraka to capture Krishna and laid siege to that city. Krishna was not in the city and when he returned, he saw the situation and fought with Sālva and killed him.

Sāmba

Sāmba was the son of Krishna and Jāmbavati. When Sāmba was a little boy Nārada came to visit Krishna. Sāmba did not get up and pay respects to Nārada. An angry Nārada decided to teach him a lesson. When Krishna was playing in the pool with his favorite wives, Nārada asked Sāmba to announce his visit. When Sāmba ran to tell Krishna about it, Krishna became angry with Sāmba for invading his privacy. He cursed Sāmba to become a leper, but he would be healthy again by bathing in Ganga at Kāshi.

Sāmba was in love with Duryodhana's daughter and so went to Hastināpuram to get her. The Kauravas did not like it and they captured him and tied him with ropes. Balarāma heard of this news and he went to Hastināpuram and threatened to destroy it unless they released Sāmba and also gave him Duryodhana's daughter. The Kauravas were afraid of Balarāma and so obliged
240

him as he wished releasing Sāmba and marrying him off with Lakshana, Duryodhana's daughter.

Sāvitri

Sāvitri was the daughter of Aswapati and Mālavi. She was raised in great comfort and educated by reputable gurus. When she became of age, her father asked her whom she would like to marry and she replied she would marry Satyavanta, son of Dyumatsena and no one else. Satyavanta had a curse on him that he would die one year after his marriage. Regardless, Sāvitri was set on the union and the marriage soon took place. Dyumatsena lost his kingdom and was forced to live in the forest. Sāvitri moved along with her husband to the forest and faithfully served him and the in-laws. She knew when the end would come, so four days before she started fasting and began prayers to all the gods. On the day Satyavanta was to die, he started to gather some firewood and fallen fruit. Sāvitri insisted she would go along with him in spite of his protest that she was weak from fasting. As they gathered the wood, Satyavanta felt tired and wanted to rest. Sāvitri knew the end was near and let him rest on her lap. Suddenly she saw someone approaching, so she gently put her husband's head down, got up, and asked the approaching person who he was. The person replied "I am Yama and I came to take your husband's life. He was such a good person that I personally came instead of sending my helpers. You may go home now." As Yama was going away with Satyavanta's life, Sāvitri followed Yama. After some time Yama asked her, why she was following him instead of going home. Sāvitri replied "I will follow my husband wherever he goes and that is the best thing I can do".

Yama took pity and asked her for anything except her husband's life. She asked that her in-laws have their eyesight and their kingdom back. This wish was granted and still Sāvitri followed Yama. After a few more steps, Yama asked her to wish another wish but not her husband's life. This time she wished that her parents would have more children and that they would be sons. That wish too was granted and then Yama reached the river Vaitarini. At that point he admonished Sāvitri that no human being could cross the river Vaitarini and she should turn back and go home. Sāvitri replied that for any woman following her husband there could be no obstacles, and also since she was in the company of Yama what if anything at all could happen to her. At that point Yama was surprised at her tenacity and granted her another wish, this time not excluding her husband's life. Sāvitri promptly asked for her husband's life and when she returned Satyavanta was up sitting and yawning as if he had just woken up. When they went back to their forest home, her in-laws got their sight back and could see what a beautiful daughter-in-law they had. They also regained their kingdom and made Satyavanta the king.

Sagara

Sagara was a king who had no children even though he had two wives. When he prayed to Shiva, he was granted many children, in fact sixty thousand with one of his wives and one with the other. Sagara wanted to express his gratitude to the gods and so embarked on a great horse sacrifice ritual. As the horse was sent, it was kidnapped by Indra and hidden behind the ashram of Kapila. Sagara's sons searched and searched and finally found the horse. They accused Kapila of stealing it. Annoyed and angry, Kapila destroyed all sixty thousand sons of Sagara with one scorching blink. Sagara heard the news from Nārada and sent his grandson to retrieve the horse from Kapila. Because all of his sons were consumed by the anger of Kapila, Sagara finished the sacrifice and left the kingdom to his grandson. His great-grandson was Bhagīratha who was determined to get all of his great uncles to heaven by bringing Ganga to flow over their ashes. After all of his sons died, Sagara prayed to the oceans and adopted them as sons. This is why oceans are also called Sāgaras. (see Bhagīratha and Ganga)

Saindhava

Saindhava was the son of the King of Sindh, Vruddhakshatra. His original name was Jayadradha. He was born with a curse that his head would be severed when he was most unprepared in battle. Knowing this, his father was saddened and put a curse on the one who would kill him "from whomever his head falls to the ground, that person's head will shatter into a hundred pieces". Jayadradha assumed the name Saindhava and married Duryodhana's sister Dussala. One day he saw Draupadi and was taken by her beauty. He approached her and asked her to marry him. When she said she was already married, he assaulted her and kidnapped her. The Pāndavas learned of this and went in pursuit of him. After defeating Saindhava, they spared his life but shaved his head and let him go. With the shame hanging on him, he went to the banks of Ganga and prayed to Shiva. When Shiva appeared, he asked to defeat all of the Pāndavas in a battle. Shiva granted the wish to come true for one day only, with the exception that he could not defeat Arjuna. When Abhimanya was fighting and expecting help, Saindhava attacked the other Pāndavas, and held them in defeat. Arjuna was fighting somewhere else and thus could not come to help his son Abhimanya. After Abhimanya was killed Arjuna was bitter and angry, so he vowed that he would slay Saindhava before the next sunset or he would renounce his weapons. This was a major vow and the Kauravas hid Saindhava in a secret place out of Arjuna's sight. The day was passing and there was no sign of Saindhava. At this point Krishna created the illusion of sunset and thinking that it was real, Saindhava and his friends came out to celebrate. The illusion was cleared and soon Arjuna felled Saidhava's head with his arrow and saw to it that it would fly far enough to land on the lap of his father. When Vruddhakshatra saw his son's head in his lap, he dropped it and according to his own curse his head cracked into several pieces.

Sairandhri

Sairandhri was Draupadi's adopted name during the year of incognito.

Samgnya

Samgnya was the daughter of Viswakarma. She married Sun and had a son Yama and a daughter Yamuna. She could not bear Sun's heat and so left her shadow, Chāya with Sun and went to her parents' home. She was told by her father to go back to her husband. Samgnya chose not to and instead went into the forests.

Sun soon found out and came to see her in the form a horse. She recognized her husband right away and they made love. Two sons were born of this adventure and they are Aswinis. (see Aswinis)

Sampāti

Sampāti was a vulture and brother of Jatāyuvu. They were powerful birds and one day they tried to reach the Sun. As they were approaching the Sun the heat was scorching their feathers and Sampāti was protecting his brother from the Sun. In that process his feathers were burned and he fell. He reached a nearby cave where he took refuge. One day while searching for Sīta, Hanumān and several monkeys came upon the cave and Sampāti was eager to make a good meal out of them. When he heard their conversation in which the name Jatāyuvu was mentioned, he asked them who they were and what had happened to his brother. Hearing how Jatāyuvu was killed by Rāvana, he decided to help Rāma and told them how Rāvana kidnapped Sīta and took her away to Lanka. He got his wings back and helped Rāma.

Sanaka, Sanandana, Santkumara

Sanaka, Sanandana, and Santkumara were sons of Brahma through meditation. They were the first maharishis. Brahma urged them to create the universe, but they refused preferring to stay in the presence of Brahma. (see Brahma)

Sanjaya

Sanjaya was the son of a charioteer in the court of Dhrutarāshtra and he served the blind king well. He was very well behaved and also fond of the Pāndavas. When they (the Pāndavas) finished their year of incognito, Sanjaya was sent as a messenger of peace, nevertheless war materialized. Sanjaya was given a special gift from Vyasa that he could see and hear others while they could not see him. He could see, hear, and describe everything in great detail to Dhrutarāshtra. He could tell what Krishna said to Arjuna in the form of Bhagavadgīta. Sanjaya could also give detailed reports on how the war was going under the commands of Bhīshma, Drōna, Karna, and finally how Duryodhana was killed. He followed Dhrutarāshtra to the forests and perished with him when they were all consumed in a raging forest fire.

Saraswati

Saraswati was the wife of Brahma and the goddess of learning. She was always seen with a Vīna. When Brahma told Shiva that he had seen the end of the universe. This was of course a lie so Shiva cursed Brahma's speech which caused Saraswati to become a river. This was one of the three rivers Ganga, Yamuna, and Saraswati.

Sarayu

Sarayu was a river near Ayodhya in which Rāma and Lakshmana drowned ending the incarnation. This was formed directly from the lake Mānasarovar near Kailas and flowed into Ganga.

Sati

Sati was the eldest daughter of Daksha and the first wife of Shiva. When Daksha was performing a great sacrifice, he invited all of the dignitaries and his daughters but not Sati. Sati was sad and wanted to go anyway in spite of Shiva's objections. When she arrived Daksha ignored her, then humiliated her by addressing her as the beggar's wife. Sati was angry and in a rage jumped into the fire and killed herself. The news reached Shiva and an angry Shiva took out one of his hairs and created Vīrabhadra ordering him to go to Daksha and destroy him and his sacrifice. Vīrabhadra went and demolished Daksha and many other attendees of his sacrifice including the Sun and Moon. Sati reincarnated as Pārvati and became Shiva's wife again.

Satrajit

Satrajit was the son of Nimna. One day he was praying to the Sun during sunrise, and a pleased Sun appeared and gave him the jewel Syamantaka. Krishna wanted the jewel and so asked Satrajit to give it to him. Instead of giving it to Krishna, Satrajit gave it to his brother Prasena who wore it for a lion hunt. The lion killed him and stole the jewel. Jāmbavanta killed the lion and got the jewel. Satrajit blamed Krishna and was spreading rumors that Krishna was a jewel thief. At that point an angry Krishna set out to find the jewel, fought with Jāmbavanta, and finally obtained the jewel. When Krishna gave it back to Satrajit, he realized what had happened, apologized, and gave his daughter Satyabhāma to Krishna along with the jewel.

Satyabhāma

Satyabhāma was the daughter of Satrajit and wife of Krishna. She aided Krishna in slaying Naraka. After hearing of Krishna's death, she retired to the forest.

Satyavanta

Satyavanta was the son of Dyumatsena who lost his kingdom and became blind. Satyavanta went to the forest to serve his parents. He married princess Sāvitri who accompanied him to the forest, although she knew that her husband would die one year after their marriage. When the time came, she pleaded with Yama and her husband was restored to life. After that they regained their kingdom and Satyavanta ruled fairly for a long time. (see Sāvitri)

Satyavati

Satyavati was the adopted daughter of Dasaraj. She was conceived when a fish swallowed the sperm of Suparichara (vasuvu).   The fish was caught by a fisherman who found Satyavati in the fish, and gave her as a gift to Dasaraj who had no children.   One day when she was ferrying people on the river Yamuna, Parāsura came and fell in love with her.   The result of their love making was a son Vyasa who grew up instantly and was very learned in all the Vedas and Sāstras.   Her son Vyasa left Satyavati right away promising to appear whenever she called for him.   After some time the king Santana came and he too fell in love with Satyavati, but he could not ask for her hand as he had a son Bhīshma.   Bhīshma approached Dasaraj and asked for Satyavati as a bride for his father.   Satyavati bore two sons with Santana, Chitrāngada and Vichitravīrya who married Ambika and Ambālika. (see Mahabhārata) When they were widowed early in their lives, Satyavati called for Vyasa, who fathered Dhrutarāshtra and Pāndu.   Satyavati knew from Vyasa that sons of Dhrutarāshtra would become bad and eventually destroy the dynasty, so she left for the forests with Ambika and Ambālika.

Satyavati (2)

Satyavati (2) was the daughter of Gādhi and wife of Ruchika. She served her husband most obligingly and he asked her for two wishes. She wished to have a son and also her mother should have a son. Those two wishes were granted, but they would have to do some special rituals and eat two different fruits each. By mistake Satyavati ate the fruit that her mother should have eaten. At that point Ruchika said that though she was a Brahmin, her son would have the straits of a Kshatriya. When Satyavati begged him not her son but her grandson should have that strait, it was granted. Thus Ruchika and Satyavati had Jamadagni as a son and

Jamadangni's son was Parasurāma who was the great martial arts guru.

Sīta

Sīta was the daughter of Janaka and the wife of Rāma. She was found in a box while the ground was being plowed. Janaka brought her to his palace and raised her. When she became of age, she was a very beautiful woman and also one of the strongest. She could easily raise Shiva's bow and span it. Janaka proclaimed "whoever can lift and span this heavy bow, that one will become Sīta's husband". Needless to say many princes tried and could not even move it. Then came Rāma accompanied by Viswaamitra and at his urging lifted the bow and tried to span it, but it broke. Sīta became the wife of Rāma. When Rāma had to go to the forest, Sīta went with him and was kidnapped by Rāvana. Rāma gathered an army of monkeys and bears under the leadership of Hanuman, Sugrīva, and Jāmbavanta and crossed the ocean into Lanka. There Rāma killed Rāvana and got Sīta back. (see Rāmayana)

In order to save his reputation from a scandal, Rāma sent Sīta away to the forest even though she was pregnant. Vālmīki took care of her and her twin sons. When Rāma finally saw the children and felt a special affection for them, they were introduced to him as his sons and just at that moment Sīta prayed to Earth which then split open and Sīta disappeared into it.

Sharadwanta

Sharadwanta was the son of Gautama. Instead of studying the Vedas, he studied the martial arts. Once he was performing tapas so intensely that Indra was afraid of him. Indra sent a beautiful woman, Janapadi to distract him. When Sharadwanta saw Janapadi he fell in love with her. At the same time he realized that she was there only to distract him. Sharadwanta went away to continue his tapas, but as a result of his love for Janapadi a son and a daughter were born. One day Sanatana came hunting, saw these two little ones, and took them with him. They were Krupa and Krupi. Krupi became the wife of Drōna.

Shalihotra

Shalihotra was a great rishi who was an expert in the science of horses. He created a pond and a tree in his ashram. Whoever drank from that pond would no longer have hunger or thirst, and whoever sat under the tree would not experience the Sun or the rain. He was the host for the Pāndavas when they came by, and he taught the science of horses to Nakula.

Shiva

Shiva was one of the three supreme gods Brahma, Vishnu, and Shiva. Shiva had no incarnations. He lived in Kailas with his wife Pārvati. He had three eyes, the third was on his forehead. When Shiva's third eye was open, whatever was in its line of sight would be annihilated. Brahma and Vishnu were debating who was greater between them, so they approached Shiva. Shiva became a lingam and asked them to find the beginning and the end of that lingam. Brahma and Vishnu went out in different ways and

Brahma thought he found it and told Shiva. Shiva knew it was a lie and so cursed Brahma. (see Brahma)

The Devas and the Danavas churned the milky ocean to obtain nectar and many other gifts. Along with those gifts such as Lakshmi, Airāvata, and the Apsaras, came Hālāhala the all-consuming fiery poison. Everyone was trying to run away from it and they all prayed to Shiva. Shiva swallowed it, but kept it in his throat because he had other worlds in his stomach. (see Hālāhala) This tarnished Shiva's neck and so he is also called Nīlakantha.

Shiva's first wife was Sati, the eldest daughter of Daksha. She came to one of his great sacrifices uninvited and was humiliated by Daksha. She jumped into the fire and killed herself. When Shiva received the sad news, he was angry and created Vīrabhadra and ordered him to demolish Daksha and his sacrifice and all those attending it. Thus the mighty Vīrabhadra went and destroyed Daksha by ripping his head, he kicked the Sun in the mouth until a few teeth fell out. He ringed the moon until he was bent, and all such deeds. Finally when Brahma begged, Shiva called off Vīrabhadra. (see Sati)

Shiva was lonely without a wife, so all of the Devas pleaded with Himavanta to have a daughter and offer her to Shiva as his wife. That daughter was Pārvati, who later served Shiva and married him. They had a son born via Agni, Ganga and found in the sawgrass and that was Kumāraswamy. They had another son Ganesha created by Pārvati. (see Ganesha)

When Vishnu came as the most beautiful woman (Jaganmohini),

253

Shiva fell in love with her and chased her until he ejaculated. When he realized that it was all an illusion, he prayed to Vishnu and asked for forgiveness. (see Jaganmohini)

Among Brahma, Vishnu, and Shiva who was the greatest? That was the question the rishis wanted to answer. They sent Bhrugu to find out. He came to Kailas when Shiva and Pārvati were playing and Shiva got angry with Bhrugu for coming without first announcing himself. Bhrugu said to Shiva: "you have more rajas in you and so you are not the greatest. Henceforth your body will not be worshipped". That is why Shiva is always represented as Lingam and not as a body.

When Bhagīratha brought Ganga to earth to save the souls of his ancestors, he prayed to Shiva to hold Ganga on his head and let him down gently. This is why Shiva wears Ganga on his head in his bushy hair. (see Ganga and Bhagīratha)

Sibi

Sibi was the son of Usīnara and Mādhavi. He ruled his kingdom without enemies and the people were happy and peaceful. Sibi was most respected for protecting whoever came seeking protection. One day Agni and Indra wanted to test him. They came as a dove and a falcon, the latter chasing the former. The dove came first and asked Sibi for protection from the falcon. Sibi promised to protect the dove. The falcon too approached him a few moments later and said "You are known for your fairness sir, this dove is my food. You cannot take away my food simply because it came first and asked for protection". Sibi replied "Yes

254

it may be your food, but choose another one and I shall give that as your food", to which the falcon demanded "In that case please give me your meat equal to the weight of this dove". Sibi agreed to that and put the dove on one side of the scale and began slicing his thigh and placing the flesh on the other side of the scale. He was slicing and slicing, but the dove side was still sinking. Finally he thought there must be something different about this dove and sat himself on the other side of the scale implying the falcon to have him as its meal. At that point both Agni and Indra took their original form, healed Sibi, and blessed him. Sibi is also known as one of the four great givers (along with Bali, Karna and Puru)

Sikhandi

Sikhandi was Amba reincarnated as a eunuch to kill Bhīshma.

Simhabala

Simhabala was the eldest of the Kīchakas and the brother of Sudheshna. He was fascinated by Draupadi and desired her very much. Bhīma plotted with Draupadi to meet with him and in darkness squeezed and killed him.

Somanādha (also called

Somasekhara)

Somanādha was another name of Shiva meaning he who wears the Moon in his head.

Subāha

Subāha was the son of Tātaka and the brother of Māricha. They were constantly disturbing the yagnas of Viswāmitra. Viswāmitra asked Dasaradha to send Rāma and Lakshmana to him to save his yagna by killing Subāha. After this Māricha avenged his brother by coming as a young deer *(bambi)* and helping Rāvana kidnap Sīta. (see Rāma, Rāvana and Lakshmana)

Subhadra

Subhadra was the daughter of Rohini and Vasudeva and the half-sister of Krishna. Although she never saw Arjuna, she heard of his greatness and fell in love with him. However her other brother Balarāma was not in favor of being related to the Pāndavas, so he promised Subhadra to Sisupāla. Before Sisupāla could come and claim Subhadra, Krishna had already arranged her marriage with Arjuna at a time when Balarāma was out on an expedition. Arjuna was hesitant to introduce Subhadra to Draupadi, but they had gotten along well because Subhadra paid her respects to Draupadi. Subhadra had a son with Arjuna called Abhimanya. (see Abhimanya)

Sudarsana

Sudarsana was the wheel of Vishnu. With this wheel Vishnu solved many crises. Sudarsana was given to Krishna by Agni when he was consuming the Khāndava forest.

Sudarsana (2)

Sudarsana (2) was the son of Agni. He had a son Oghavanta and his daughter was Oghāvati, who married her grandfather. Sudarsana wanted to conquer death by never refusing the desires of any guest. One day Yama came as a guest and after enjoying Sudarsana's hospitality desired to make love to Oghāvati. While they were intimate, Sudarsana called for Oghāvati and she did not answer. Then he looked to see what was going on and Yama replied that his wife was pleasing him. Sudarsana calmly replied "if my guest is pleased that is all I ever wanted". At that moment Yama assumed his true form and assured him that he had conquered death.

Sudheshna

Sudheshna was the wife of Bali. She was asked to have children by Dīrghatama, but instead of her having children, she sent her servant to Dīrghatama. Bali thought first they were his children, when Dīrghatama said they were not. Bali asked her a second time to go to Dīrghatama; this time she obliged and had a powerful son called Anga. (see Bali)

Sudheshna (2)

Sudheshna(2) was the sister of Kīchaka and the wife of Virāta. She ordered Draupadi to serve his brother who had designs on her. (see Kīchaka and Mahābhārata)

Sugrīva

Sugrīva was a monkey king and the brother of Vāli. He was the son of the Sun from Ahalya. When Ahalya's husband Gautama was not in his home, Indra and Sun went to Ahalya and seduced her. She gave birth to two very powerful boys. As they were growing, Gautama thought they were his children, but his daughter told him that they were really the sons of Indra and Sun. An angry Gautama lifted the two boys and cursed them that they should have the appearance of a monkey and left them on the beach. They were taken by a rishi called Rukshavīraja who raised them. They were two very powerful brothers; Vāli was the king of Kishkindha and Sugrīva was his right hand man. One day the demon Māyavi came and challenged Vāli to a fight. Vāli fought him fiercely and followed him into a cave. Sugrīva was waiting outside, and after a short time blood was flowing from the cave. Thinking Vāli was dead and to prevent Mayavi from coming out, he closed the cave with a large boulder, went back to Kishkindha and assumed the throne. A few days later, Vāli came out after killing Māyavi, and saw Sugrīva on his throne with his wife. He accused Sugrīva of willfully scheming to take over his throne, fought him and banished him from his kingdom. Sugrīva went to Rusyamūka with his following that included Hanumān, Jāmbavanta, and their following. When Rāma appeared saearching for his wife Sīta, Hanumān introduced Rāma to Sugrīva, who promised to find Sīta if Rāma could help him kill Vāli. Rāma agreed to that condition and Sugrīva wanted to test him whether he could deliver. So he asked Rāma to show his ability by cutting down three palm trees with one arrow. In fact when Rāma attempted to do that, not three but seven trees fell at one time. That impressed Sugrīva very much and the next day he challenged Vāli to a fight. He also told Rāma that whoever fights Vāli face to face, he would loose half of his strength to Vāli. He asked Rāma to hide behind a tree and at the appropriate moment kill Vāli with his arrow. The brothers were fighting fiercely and Sugrīva was losing and fatigued, but there was no sign of Rāma killing Vāli. He got tired and ran away to Rusyamūka. There he accused Rāma of reneging on his promise. Rāma told him that he was there but could not figure out who was who, because both brothers looked the same. The next day Sugrīva wore a garland and asked Vāli to fight with him. It was easy for Rāma now to see who was Vāli and at an appropriate time when Vāli was facing the other side, Rāma shot an arrow from behind that killed Vāli. Sugrīva assumed the throne and also took Tara (Vāli 's wife), and sent the troops to search for Sīta. Hanumān flew to Lanka and found Sīta. Rāma assembled an army of monkeys and bears, and with the help of Hanumān, conquered Rāvana and took Sīta back. After that war, Sugrīva made Angada (son of Vāli) as king of Kishkindha and he himself went with Rāma to Ayodhya and stayed there for a long time and returned to Kishkindha to die.

Surya

Surya is another name for Sun.

Tāra

Tāra was the wife of Bruhaspati. Chandra (Moon) was studying under Bruhaspati and Tāra fell in love with him and bore a son Budha by him. After an intense quarrel, Brahma determined Budha as son of Chandra and gave him to Chandra and Tāra to Bruhaspati. (see Budha, Bruhaspati, and Chandra)

Tāra (2)

Tāra (2) was the wife of Vāli and mother of Angada. (see Angada)

Tātaka

Tātaka was a rakshasa woman and the mother of Mārichi and Subāha. She was destroying Viswāmitra's Yagna by pouring meats, blood, and other remains of her victims until Rāma killed her with his arrow.

Takshaka

Takshaka was the son of Kadruva and a very powerful snake. When Parīkshit was cursed by Srungi that he would be bitten by a snake and die, it was Takshaka who entered the palace through a fruit and killed Parīkshit. (see Parīkshit and Kasyapa)

Trisanku

Trisanku was a king of the Sun dynasty. His original name was Satyavrata. He kidnapped a married woman and was banished by his father to leave his kingdom. Trisanku left and there was a great famine in the kingdom for twelve years. Everyone was starving including Viswāmitra. He saved Viswāmitra by giving him food. His father's resident priest was Vasishta who had the sacred cow. Satyavrata killed the cow to feed Viswāmitra, but he ate the cow meat first. Vasishta cursed him to have three stakes in his heart, one for offending his father, another for killing the cow of the guru, and and a third for eating the cow meat. He then became Trisanku. He was married to Satyaradha and their son was Harischandra.

After Trisanku assumed the throne, he wanted to perform a sacrifice to go to heaven directly. He asked Vasishta to be the chief priest to perform that yagna. Vasishta refused and he next asked Viswāmitra who agreed, but none of the great rishis came for the yagna. Viswāmitra performed it single handedly and sent Trisanku to heaven. Indra refused to admit him to heaven and actually pushed him down. As he was falling, he cried for Viswāmitra who stopped him midway between heaven and earth and threatened to create a new heaven for him. Indra protested but in the end agreed for Trisanku to stay where he was between earth and heaven.

Tulasi

Tulasi was the daughter of Dharmadhwāja and Mādhavi. She went to Badari and prayed to Brahma and when Brahma appeared and asked for her wish, she replied that she would like to become the wife of Vishnu. Brahma agreed to this but said to her that she would also be cursed by Vishnu and become a tree. He said she would be one of the great pativratas and even as a tree you woud be revered. Somewhat disappointed, she was wandering in the forest when Sankhachuda saw her and fell in love with her. At the same time Nārada came by and convinced them that they would make a great couple and married them off. Sankhachuda was a powerful man and he fought all of the Devas. There was no one that could defeat him, Kali tried and failed as did Kumāraswamy. Finally Shiva came and killed Sankhachuda and took his armor. Shiva put on the armor and went to Tulasi. Tulasi thought it was her husband and was serving him when she suddenly realized that this man was not Sankhachuda. Shiva was afraid at first and then explained to her that he and Vishnu were the same and her desire was fulfilled. Since then Tulasi became a tree and every Hindu family has at least one tulasi plant in their homes. Tulasi became a holy plant.

Uchaiswara

Uchaiswara was the white horse of Indra. Uchaiswara was the reason for the quarrel between Kadruva and Vinata. (see Kadruva,

Vinata, and Garuda)

Uma

Uma was another name for Pārvati.

Urmila

Urmila was the cousin of Sīta and wife of Lakshmana. When Lakshmana went with Rāma, Urmila did not go with them. Instead she slept all the time so that Lakshmana did not have to sleep. Thus Laksmana could kill Kumbhakarna because he could only be killed by one who had not slept for fourteen years.

Urvasi

Urvasi was one of the Apsaras. When Nara and Nārayana were deeply involved in their tapas, Indra sent some apsaras to disturb them. They went there and were making lots of noise, when Nārayana opened his eyes and scratched his thigh from which came a more beautiful maiden than any of the apsaras. They were ashamed and left. After seeing Urwasi, Indra promptly claimed her and made her chief apsara. *(Thigh is called Uru in Sanskrit, because she was born from the thigh with the name Urvasi).*

Usha

Usha was the daughter of Bana. She was Tilottama in a previous life. One day she saw a handsome prince in her dream and made love with him. When she related the story to Chitrarēkha (one of her confidantes), she sought pictures of all the princes and showed them to Usha. She recognized Aniruddha as the one whom she saw in her dream. Aniruddha was a cousin of Krishna and lived in Dwāraka. He was taken secretly to Bana's palace and when he saw Usha, he fell in love with her. They lived secretly for sometime until Usha became pregnant. When Bana heard of the pregnancy, he immediately chained Aniruddha and released him only after Krishna fought him and defeated him. A son called Vajra was born to Usha and Aniruddha.

Uttanapada

Uttanapada was the father of Dhruva and son of Swāyambhuva manu. (see Dhruva)

Uttara

Uttara was the son of Virāta who liked to boast that he could easily defeat the Kauravas and release the hostage cows. When Uttara actually had to fight the Kauravas, he wanted to run. Arjuna convinced him that they could fight the Kauravas together and they did. This was the reason for the expression boasting like Uttara, meaning empty boasting.

Uttara (2)

Uttara (2) was the daughter of Virāta. She became the wife of Abhimanya and their son was Parīkshit. (see Arjuna)

Vāli

Vāli was the brother of Sugrīva and the son of Ahalya and Surya. Indra and Surya (Sun) fell in love with Ahalya and when her husband was not at home seduced her and both made love to her. She gave birth to two very powerful sons and Guatama was thinking they were his sons. His daughter told him the truth and he was angry and left the boys on the shores of the ocean. (see Sugrīva) Vāli was the most powerful king of his day and ruled Kishkindha. He was a fair ruler and his brother Sugrīva was his right hand man. One day the demon Māyavi came by and challenged Vāli to a fight. He even ridiculed Vāli by saying that he would wait until Vāli finished his sleep with his wives because he may not be able to again after fighting with him. Vāli was incensed and the fight began immediately. The fight was fierce because Māyavi was full of tricks, but they were no match for Vāli. As the fight progressed, Māyavi suddenly entered into a cave and Vāli followed him. Outside Sugrīva and others were waiting. Blood was slowly flowing from the cave and the noises suddenly subsided. Sugrīva thought Vāli was dead and did not wish Māyavi to come out and destroy Kishkindha. He pushed a large boulder in front of the entrance to the cave and returned to the palace. He relayed the news and was given the throne. Sugrīva also took Vāli's wife Tāra. In the mean time Vāli struggled to push the stone and when he finally came out and saw what happened, he accused Sugrīva of planning all this to take the throne and his wife. He banished him from his kingdom.

One day Vāli was bathing in the ocean and Rāvana climbed on his shoulders to scare him. Vāli caught him as he would catch a mosquito and dipped him repeatedly in the water until Rāvana begged him for mercy. Vāli was also married to Mandōdari (Rāvana's wife) and had a son Angada with her.

When Rāma killed Vāli from behind, Vāli asked him why he had killed him, and in such an unworthy manner for a king. Rāma consoled him and promised to make Angada king after Sugrīva.

266

(see Rāma, Mandōdari, and Angada)

Vālmīki

Vālmīki was the first poet who wrote the Rāmayana in verse form. He was actually a son of Brahma accidentally born when Brahma fell in love with one of the apsaras. Vālmīki went to Brahma and confronted him to recognize his birth. Brahma became angry and cursed him to be a thug and untouchable on earth. When Vālmīki begged for mercy, Brahma said he would be relieved of the curse when he sees Rāma and writes the story of Rāmayana. Vālmīki became a thug and a bandit robbing innocent travelers to feed his family. One day the seven rishis happened to come by and Vālmīki attacked them for what little they were carrying. One of the rishis said to Vālmīki that he was committing a great deal of sin in order to feed his family, and asked whether his family would share in bearing the punishment for his sins. Vālmīki had no answer, then the rishis urged him to find out and they would wait until he returned. Vālmīki went home and asked his wife and children whether they would share his sins. They said no, it was his responsibility to feed his family and whatever sins he committed in doing so, they were his sins. A puzzled Vālmīki came back to the rishis and told what his family had said and begged them to teach him how to purify himself. The rishis gave him a mantra of Rāma and asked him to utter that. A repenting Vālmīki sat down, closed his eyes, and began the mantra. He sat perfectly still and after some time a pile of earth grew on him and a few trees around him. Such a pile of earth is called Vālmīkam in Sanskrit and thus the name Vālmīki. Vishnu was going to be incarnated as Rāma. Nārada heard this and was asked not to disclose it to anyone. Nārada could not keep it to himself and so instead of telling this to anybody, he told the story of Rāma to the trees around Vālmīki and Vālmīki heard it. One day Vālmīki was returning from the river with his pupils and he saw a hunter killing a bird during mating. He asked the hunter why he had commited this cruel act and that was the first rhyme in Sanskrit. This is why Vālmīki is also known as the first poet (ādi Kavi). He later composed the entire Ramāyana in verse form which was also an epic.

When Rāma abandoned Sīta and sent her away to the forest, it was Vālmīki who gave her shelter and gave the names Lava and Kusa to her children and educated them. When they went to Rāma and sang the story of Rāmayana, Rāma was so moved that a crying Rāma asked the boys to take him to Sīta. When he saw Sīta, she bowed to his feet and she disappeared into the ground. (see Sīta, Rāma, and Rāmayana)

Vāmana

Vāmana was the fifth incarnation of Vishnu as a dwarf Brahmin sent to crush Bali and restore the heavens to Indra. (see Bali)

Vātapi

Vātapi was the brother of Ilvala. The brothers were disappointed in Brahmins because they would not give them what they wanted, namely a mantra to achieve anything they desired. Thus angry with all Brahmins, they began killing them. Vātapi would become

268

a goat and Ilavla would cook it and feed his Brahmin guests. Then he would call loudly Vātapi "where are you, please come to your brother" and Vātapi would come out tearing the bellies of the Brahmins. After hearing this, Agastya went to Ilvala and soon after dinner before Ilvala could call for his brother, rubbed his belly saying "digest Vātapi digest" and that was Vātapi's end. (see Agastya and Ilvala)

Vāyu

Vāyu was one of the eight rulers of the directions and had the form of wind. Actually he was a Brahmin by the name of Putātma and was a colleague of Kasyapa. He went to Kāshi and prayed to Shiva and a pleased Shiva made him ruler of the Northeast. Vāyu is known for his strength. Once when he saw Brahma, he boasted that he could lift and whirl anything and Brahma asked him to lift a blade of grass and Vāyu could not. He then recognized Brahma and paid respects to him. He had a son with Anjana (see Anjanēya or Hanumān) and another with Kunti. (see Bhīma and Kunti)

Vaikuntha

Vishnu's abode was filled with all the comforts of the world such as lakes, ponds, flower paths, and cool places. All the sages and rishis visited Vaikuntha to see Vishnu and enjoy his hospitality. The gatekeepers of Vaikuntha were Jaya and Vijaya. They were cursed by the rishis and when they begged for mercy they were told to become either enemies of Vishnu for three incarnations or friends for seven. They chose to be enemies for they wanted to return to Vaikuntha as soon as possible. Those enemies were Hiranyāksha and Hiranyakasipa (killed by Varāha and Narasimha), Rāvana and Kumbhakarna (killed by Rāma and Lakshmana), and Kamsa and Sisupāla (killed by Krishna).

Varāha

Varāha was a boar and the third incarnation of Vishnu. (see Hiranyāksha)

Varuna

Varuna was the son of Kardama and the ruler of the west. He was also the lord of the seas. As the son of Kardama he was named Suchishmanta. As a little boy Suchishmanta was swallowed by a crocodile and taken to the oceans. When the ocean knew who he was, he was sent back to his father who then asked him to go to Kāshi and pray to Shiva. Suchishmanta did this and Shiva was pleased with his prayers. Shiva made him the ruler of the west and gave Suchishmanta the name Varuna.

Vasishta

Vasishta was one of the seven rishis. One day Varuna and Surya (Sun) were walking and saw Urvasi. They both experienced ejaculation and Urvasi stored their sperm in a pot from which was born Agastya and Vasishta. He married Arundhati and had several children. His grandson was Parāsara. One day King

Viswāmitra came by after a hunt and Vasishta treated him and his entourage to a sumptuous meal provided by Kāmadhēnu (the holy cow). Viswāmitra was surprised at the powers of the cow and asked Vasishta to give it to him in lieu of a thousand cows. Vasishta refused and so Viswāmitra tried to take the cow by force when an army of soldiers came from the cow and defeated Viswāmitra. Viswāmitra realized that such powers could come only from tapas and started on tapas of his own. He prayed and prayed and Brahma came and called him rājarshi but he did not stop until Vasishta himself came and called him brahmarshi thus making Viswamitra a Brahmin. All the time Vasishta and Viswāmitra were rivals.

In the court of Indra, a question arose if there was anyone who had never told a lie or reneged on his word. Vasishta pointed out that such a person existed and his name was Harischandra. Viswāmitra immediately vowed that he would make Harischandra tell a lie, and created many hardships for him, although finally conceded that he could not make Harischandra tell a lie. (see Harischandra)

Vasishta was the resident priest of the Sun dynasty and helped perform many sacrifices by Ikshwaka, and Dasaradha.

Vasudeva

Vasudeva was the father of Krishna and the husband of Devaki. His brother-in-law Kamsa heard that he would be killed by the offspring of Vasudeva and Devaki, so he wanted to kill them right away. Vasudeva begged him to spare his wife and in return he

271

would deliver all of his children as soon as they were born. Kamsa agreed to this and put them in jail. When the eighth child was born, Vasudeva quickly gave that infant to Yasoda who had just given birth to a baby girl. He took the baby girl and gave her to Kamsa.(see Kamsa, Devaki, and Krishna)

Vasudeva had other wives one of which was Rohini, the mother of Balarāma. In a previous life Vasudeva was Kasyapa and Aditi was Devaki. (see Kasyapa, Aditi, and Kadruva)

Veda

The Vedas are the holy scriptures of the Hindu religion. There are four of them, one each coming out of one face of Brahma. The four are: Rigveda, Yazurveda, Adharvaveda, and Samaveda.

Vedavyāsa

Vedavyāsa was a title earned by scholarship in the Vedas and their explanations. In every period there were special scholars who became Vedavyasas. For instance Swāyambhuvu was the first Vedavyāsa. Other Vedavyāsas included Bruhaspati, Sukra, and Vasishta.

Venkateswara or Venkatesa

One day Bhrugu came to Vishnu and argued with him in an abrasive manner and even insulted him. When Vishnu did not
272

react to the insults, his wife Lakshmi got angry and left him for a short while and went to Kollapuram. Vishnu felt lonely and went to the mountain Sehadri and hid in an anthill as Venkateswara. Lakshmi heard this and wanted to help him. She consulted Shiva and Brahma and they both became a cow and calf. Lakshmi took the cow and calf and sold them to King Chola. Everyday the cow was going to the anthill and pouring all her milk on the anthill for Venkatesa. When there was no milk Chola angrily accused the cowboy of stealing the milk. On the next day the cowboy went along with the cow and saw what was happening. He took his ax and was about to chop the anthill when Vishnu popped his head out and received the blow. The cow (Shiva) was about to curse the cowboy, but was prevented by Vishnu. After all it was Vishnu's fault and not that of the cowboy. They all sought the help of Bruhaspati to heal the wound and he prescribed a special leaf for the healing. As Venkatesa was searching for this leaf, he was tired and taken in by a matron called Vakulamāli who found the leaf and nurtured him too. Venkatesa was always depressed and when asked why, he replied that he was in love with the King's daughter Padmāvati. Vakulamāli went to Padmāvati and found out that she too was in love with Venkatesa and diplomatically arranged for the marriage. However, she did not know how Lakshmi would take all this, and so sent Surya (Sun) to find out. Lakshmi did not object and Venkatesa married Padma. A temple was built in their honor near that place which is today called Tirupati. *(Venkateswara temples are also in the USA now, one in Pittsburgh, Pennsylavania and a few others spread around the country.)* Venkateswara is also known as Bālaji (meaning boy god).

Vibhīshana

Vibhīshana was the brother of Rāvana. When Rāma went to Lanka to wage a war over Sīta, it was Vibhīshana who advised Rāvana to give Sīta back to Rāma and ask for his forgiveness. Rāvana became infuriated and asked Vibhīshana to leave Lanka. Vibhīshana left Lanka and asked for shelter with Rāma. First they thought he was a spy sent by Rāvana but then found out the truth and accepted him. During the battle, it was Vibhīshana who disclosed some secret positions of Lanka and also about the special sacrifice Rāvana was performing and asked Rāma to stop it any way possible because if it was completed, Rāvana would be unconquerable. Rāma sent Angada who dragged Mandōdari to Rāvana. An infuriated Rāvana broke off the sacrifice, and went to battle Rāma. Also when Rāvana's heads kept coming back after every slaying, it was Vibhīshana who told Rāma the secret of Rāvana holding nectar in his navel and suggested that Rāma first aim at Rāvana's navel. Thus without Vibhīshana, Rāma could not have killed Rāvana. When the battle was over, Vibhīshana was installed as king of Lanka and he gave Rāma the Pushpaka, Rāvana's flying chariot. Vibhīshana was actually only a half-brother of Rāvana.

Vichitravīrya

Vichitravīrya was the son of Satyavati and Santana and the half-brother of Bhīshma. He was married to Amba, but was killed in a fight with the gandhrvas. (see Bhīshma and Mahābhārata)

Vidura

Vidura was the son of Vyasa and the servant maid of Ambika. Both Pāndu and Dhrutarāshtra treated Vidura as their brother and always sought his advice. Vidura was actually Yama in his previous life and was born as Vidura because of a curse. (see Māndavya) Vidura was Yama and Dharmaja was Yama's son and that relationship of father and son showed all through Mahābhārata

Vighneswara

Vighneswara was another name of Ganesha. (see Ganesha)

Vijaya

Vijaya was one of the gatekeepers of Vaikuntha. The other was Jaya. When they were cursed by the visiting rishis, Vishnu gave them the choice of becoming his foe for three generations or his friend for seven generations to overcome the curse. They chose to be Vishnu's foes. (see Jaya and Vaikuntha)

Vinata

Vinata was the wife of Kasyapa and the daughter of Daksha and Dharani (Earth). She and Kadruva (another wife of Kasyapa) became pregnant at the same time and Kadruva gave birth to serpents. Vinata waited and waited and finally aborted the child when a half-formed boy came out. He cursed Vinata to become a slave of Kadruva, because she had not waited untill he was fully formed. That boy was Anūra. One day Kadruva and Vinata were walking and saw the heavenly horse Uchaisrava. Vinata said how nice and white the horse was, but Kadruva just to contradict her, commented that its tail was somewhat black. Since it was already late and the Sun had gone down, they decided to return the next day to determine who was right. In the mean time Kadruva called all her children and asked for a black snake to wind around Uchaisrava's tail just enough to make it look black. Otherwise she would have to become a servant of Vinata. If it appeared black, then Vinata would become her servant. The next day they went to see the horse and sure enough the tail looked black. Vinata became Kadruva's servant. She then gave birth to Garuda the mighty eagle, who also had to become a slave to Kadruva and the serpents. One day Garuda asked how they could be relieved from the slavery and the serpents answered that if he could bring the nectar from Indra and give it to them, then he and his mother would be free. Garuda went to Indra and conquered him. He brought back the nectar and freed Vinata from her slavery. (see Garuda and Kadruva)

Vishnu

Vishnu is one of the three principal gods, Brahma, Vishnu, and Shiva. Vishnu came as nine incarnations, the tenth one is yet to come. Every time he came to establish order (dharma) and eliminate evil. First he came as a fish to rescue the Vedas, second as a tortoise to support churning the oceans, then as a boar to kill Hiranyāksha. The fourth one was Narasimha (half-lion half-man) to destroy Hiranyakasipa. The fifth was Vāmana (dwarf Brahmin) to crush Bali. He also came as Parasurāma, Rāma, Krishna, and

277

Buddha. The tenth one Kalika (or Kalki) is yet to come. (see Brahma, and all the above names)

Viswakarma

Viswakarma was the architect and engineer of the heavens. Indra commissioned him to build many cities. One day he was traveling in his chariot and saw the apsara Ghrutāchi. He asked her to make love to him, which she refused. He cursed her to be born as a lower class woman on earth. She counter-cursed him to be born as a man of lower intellect on earth. He begged her to remove the curse. The curse could not be removed but she said he would be born as a man of formidable talent. He came as a half-Brahmin and was living on the banks of the river Yamuna. Ghrutāchi was born as a shepherd maid and saw Viswakarma. He recognized her as Ghrutāchi and they had several children who were artisans such as blacksmiths, carpenters, and metal workers.

Viswāmitra

Viswāmitra was the son of Gādhi and became king after Gādhi. One day he went hunting and grew tired and went to Vasishta's ashram. Vasishta showed them great hospitality and fed him and his entourage with the help of the holy cow (Kāmadhēnu). Viswāmitra was astonished and asked for the cow in return for a thousand other cows. Vasishta refused and when Viswāmitra tried to take it by force, his army was defeated by the soldiers from the cow. Then Viswāmitra realized it was the power that the Brahmin Vasishta had so he decided to acquire such power for

278

himself. He set out alone and began tapas. Indra wanted to distract him, and so sent Menaka. Viswāmitra fell in love with her and they had a girl and that was Sakuntala. He realized that he was distracted and went back to his tapas. Viswāmitra trained several scholars, one of which was Kālava. When he finished, Kālava asked what he could give as a gift to his guru. Viswāmitra first denied he wanted anything, but a persistant Kālava annoyed him and so he asked for eight white horses with blue ears. Kālava searched and could find only six such horses so he brought those six and also Yayāti's daughter Mādhavi. Viswāmitra accepted

them as gifts and he had a son Ashtaka from Mādhavi. There was a great famine; Viswāmitra and his family were given food and shelter by Satyavrata. Later Satyavrata performed a great sacrifice under the priestship of Viswāmitra, which was boycotted by many other rishis. Viswāmitra performed it and sent Satyavrata to heaven. Indra pushed him down saying that he did not deserve to be in heaven. Then Viswāmitra stopped him in the middle and began creating a heaven for Satyavrata. (see Trisanku) A frightened Indra accepted Trisanku as a member of the heavens although his position was in the middle.

Viswāmitra's archrival was Vasishta and he wanted Vasishta to call him Brahmarshi. He made great tapas and all of the Devas were afraid. They urged him to go to Vasishta, and when he did Vasishta addressed him as rājarshi only. An angry Viswāmitra killed one of Vasishta's sons by his powers. Some time later he came again to Vasishta and Vasishta addressed him only as rājarshi again. An angry Viswāmitra inflicted damage to another of Vasista's sons. After some time Viswāmitra came to Vasishta again and Vasishta called him rājarshi once again. This time

Viswāmitra showed no anger and simply walked away, when Vasishta called him brahmarshi please come and enjoy my hospitality. He then explained to Viswāmitra that now he has no anger and thus eligible to be called brahmarshi.

Viswāmitra bet with Vasishta on making Harischandra tell a lie. He sent his disciple who was torturing Harischandra but could not make him tell a lie. In the end when Harischandra was ordered to behead his wife, both Vasishta and Viswāmitra appeared and saved his wife. (see Harischandra)

Viswāmitra was performing a great sacrifice which was consistently disturbed by two demons Māricha and Subāha. He went to Dasaradha and asked for the, help of Rāma and Laksmana to kill the demons. He taught them the martial arts and they killed the demons and saved his sacrifice. As a reward he took them to Janaka's court where Rāma bent the bow of Shiva and married Sīta. (see Rāma, Dasaradha, Sīta, and Janaka)

Vyāsa

Vyāsa was the son of Parāsara and Satyavati. When he was born he was already a scholar in the Vedas. He gave his promise to appear whenever his mother wished, and then disappeared. Later when Satyavatis daughters-in-law Ambika and Ambālika were widowed without children, Satyavati called Vyāsa and sent Ambika and Ambālika to him. Thus were born Dhrutarāshtra and Pāndu. She also sent the servant maid to whom was born Vidura. Parāsara was a grandson of Vasishta and Vyāsa when born was named Krishnadwaipāyana, and became Vyāsa later.

Vyāsa was a great scholar and also wrote eighteen Puranas. Mahābhārata was one of them.

Yama

Yama was the son of Sun and Sangna and the lord of the netherworld and the South. He was also known as Dharma. Yama was born as Vidura because of a curse by Māndavya. Yama and Kunti had a son Dharmaja who always preserved the law.

Yasoda

Yasoda was Nanda's wife and she raised Krishna. (see Krishna) Actually she gave birth to a baby girl who was exchanged for Krishna by Vasudeva.

Yayāti

Yayāti was the king of the Chandra dynasty and the son of Nahusha. One day as he was hunting he heard cries of help from a well. He saw Devayāni in the well. Yayāti lifted her out of the well and married her. (see Devayāni and Kacha) Devayāni had a rivalry with Sarmishta who also came to Yayāti as a servant. Yayāti had three children with Devayāni and another with Sarmishta named Pūru. Devayāni got angry that her husband slept with her servant and left him for her father's home. When her father Sukra heard that his daughter had been slighted by Yayāti, he cursed Yayāti to become an old man. Yayāti begged his father-in-law to reverse the curse because he was still young and in love with his Devayāni and would very much like to enjoy his life with her. Sukra conditionally reversed the curse, saying that if he could borrow someone's youth he could be young again and that person would become old. Yayāti first asked his sons from Devayāni and they refused. He then asked Pūru who gladly obliged saying "pleasing my father is the best thing I can do". Thus Yayāti enjoyed youth for a long time and after his reign made Pūru the king. Pūru was one of the four great givers. (see Pūru and Devayāni)

The 18 Purānas

Agni Purāna
Bhāgavata Purāna
Bhavishya Purāna
Brahma Purāna
Brahmānda Purāna
Brahmavaivarta Purāna
Garuda Purāna
Kurma Purāna
Linga Purāna
Mārkandeya Purāna
Matsya Purāna
Nārada Purāna
Padma Purāna
Shiva Purāna
Skanda Purana
Vāmana Purāna
Varāha Purāna
Vishnu Purāna

Further Reading For More Details:

Vishnu Purāna - translated into English by H.H. Wilson (1840)

Mahā Bhārata of Vyāsa - translated by K.M. Ganguli (1883 –1896)

Rāmāyana of Vālmiki - translated by R.T.H. Griffith (1870 –1874)

Rāmāyana and Mahā Bhārata – abridged version by R.Dutt (1899)

Bhāgavatam – translated by Swami Vijayananda (H. P.Chatterji) (1921)

Biography

Kolluru Ramakrishna Sarma was born in Maddivalasa, a village in the state of Andhra Pradesh, India. His father was a Sanskrit scholar and a faculty in the Department of Philosophy in Andhra University. Ramakrishna graduated in Chemical Engineering from Andhra University. He then went to Karlsruhe, Germany on a German Government scholarship and earned a doctorate in

Mechanical Engineering from the Technical University, Karlsruhe. After working for a few years as an engineer and educator, Dr. Sarma came to the United States as a Professor at Old Dominion University, Norfolk, Virginia.

Dr. Sarma lived in Richmond, Virginia for many years. There he assisted the Virginia Museum of Fine Arts curator of the Indian section, Dr. Joseph M. Dye III, in translating "ASWASATRA" of Salihotra from Sanskrit. (see www.vmfa.museum) Dr. Sarma was part of a Gita study group that read and interpreted the BHAGAVADGITA. He was a frequent participant in the activities of the Hindu center and the annual India Festival.

He now lives in Alexandria, Virginia. His current interests include writing and translating Hindu religious books.

Events

Dr. Sarma is available for book discussions, classroom presentations and college lectures. He travels from the Washington, DC area airports throughout the United States. If you would like to discuss an event, please refer to the contact details below.

Contact

Dr. Sarma's agent can be reached by email at msarma222@gmail.com and voice at 804.372.7629.

Thank you for being interested in Hindu mythology.

Printed in Great Britain
by Amazon